JAMES HERBERT'S
DARK
PLACES

JAMES HERBERT'S DARK PLACES

LOCATIONS AND LEGENDS

JAMES HERBERT

PHOTOGRAPHS BY PAUL BARKSHIRE

HarperCollins*Publishers*

HarperCollins*Publishers*
77-85 Fulham Palace Road
Hammersmith, London W6 8JB

Published by HarperCollins*Publishers* 1993
1 3 5 7 9 8 6 4 2

A catalogue record for this book
is available from the British Library

ISBN 0 00 255496 8

Set in Garamond No 3

Produced by Lennard Books
a division of Lennard`Associates Limited
Mackerye End
Harpenden
Herts AL5 5DR

Design by Cooper Wilson
Editor Roderick Brown

Printed in Great Britain by
Butler and Tanner, Frome and London

ACKNOWLEDGEMENT

The publishers are grateful to the following for the use of additional photographs:
Hulton Deutsch Picture Library, the Royal Commission for Historical Monuments, the Warburg Institute,
University College Hospital, B.E.C. Howarth-Loomes and Oxford County Libraries.
Thanks also to Tom Perrott for his help in the research for this book.

CONTENTS

Novels by James Herbert

THE RATS
LAIR
DOMAIN
THE FOG
THE SURVIVOR
FLUKE
THE SPEAR
THE DARK
THE JONAH
SHRINE
MOON
THE MAGIC COTTAGE
SEPULCHRE
HAUNTED
CREED
PORTENT

Other Sources

There are many books about haunted, evil, possessed or merely mysterious and unexplained places –
some were tracked down in the almost silent recesses of the London Library; others, 150 years old
and with a faded musty scent of their own were gingerly consulted in the Guildhall Library. But
three in particular were essential; first Antony D.Hippisley Coxe's *Haunted Britain*, a meticulously
researched survey that combines prodigious knowledge with an accessible format; second, equally
valuable, is Peter Underwood's *A Gazetteer of British Ghosts*, with its excellent, detailed entries, many
based on the author's own experience, on a wide range of places graced by hauntings; and finally The
Reader's Digest book *Folklore, Myths and Legends*, well laid out and full of fascinating tales.

PROLOGUE

In this book I want to share with you places – some real, some imaginary – which reflect my imagination. Places are the backdrops, the sets, even the first inspiration of my novels. Sometimes a brief sighting can linger and grow into something that won't go away – something you *have* to write about: that unexplained window in the attic of a country house reflecting the pale autumn light; the centuries-old mystery and the mingled scents of incense, polish and, well, *age* in a mediaeval church; the cold rush of wind over a lonely beach, the hardly-moving surface of a brackish lake, teeming with...what?...below the surface. The imagination can take something real, something tangible, and use it to make new worlds of possibilities...

So places aren't just precise locations for me: they can be evocations of a mood, too. And when I came across Paul Barkshire's eerie photographs I realised that here was someone who could capture many aspects of how I use places in my stories. I didn't want to be restricted to one type of place, or any one way I'd used places – no fun for the imagination, mine or yours, in that. Instead I've looked at the idea from different perspectives that interested me. I chose some places that I've used as themselves – Eton College Chapel in *The Survivor* and – total contrast – the Lloyd's building in *Portent*; then there are the real-life inspirations behind fictional locations in my novels – warm-red brick Compton Wynyates, my source for the sinister Neath in *Sepulchre*, for example.

Paul also took photographs to capture the general ambience, the mood, of my novels. Images that make me (and you I hope) wonder what might be about to happen; scenes that seem calm, even peaceful ... yet there is something in them that makes me wonder ... for it's not necessarily the most obvious menace that lingers, but the nagging sense of doubt...

And then there are those places associated with tales that are, I suppose, our ghostly – *ghastly* – heritage. Stories of murder, torture, mystery, sadness from the past that imbue so many locations with a *something*: a cold sensation; a shivering; a sense of being watched; appearances of formless 'things' or all-too-recognisable headless or bloodied human forms. These stories tug at our minds when we least want them to – normally when we're alone in the dark – and I've included some that appeal to me.

Thanks then to Paul for braving the elements (and elementals?) to bring back so many images that combine subtle menace with real artistry. And to Roderick Brown for researching and writing the captions to those real places with terrible tales of their own; to Adrian Stephenson and Paul Cooper for excellent production and design on a crazy schedule; and to Malcolm Edwards at Harper Collins.

INTRODUCTION

I like a graveyard on a sunny day. I like the drone of a bee, the trill of a bird, perhaps even the distant sounds of children at play, as I wander down thin paths cut through burial mounds. I remember standing among gravestones once and hearing the *thwack* of leather on willow as a cricket match progressed in the field next door to the cemetery. I enjoy these proclamations of life intruding upon the deadness of the graveyard.

No need for dark brooding skies; sunlight on a sepulchre provides mood enough. No need for rain lashing lichen-diseased tombstones when withered and brittle flowers laid beneath a stone-curved legend tender their own grim ambience. Forget the howling wind, the far-off cry of a frightened animal, the heavy footsteps of some unseen person: just give me a graveyard on a bright summer's day and leave the rest to my own evocations. Let me conjure a figure, perhaps dressed in black or in a shroud, standing there in the middle-distance. Quiet and still. Watching...

Burial places have that fascination for me, as do old dwellings, gothic churches, lakes and marshlands. Lonely places whose very stillness allows the imagination full-flight. I revel in the legends of such locations, feel inspired by their atmosphere. They become strong elements of my stories – my plays, if you like – whether used as props, backdrops or presented centre-stage, and they lend credibility to the incredible, a factual basis for the fiction built around them.

Naturally, the more eerie a place is, the more I'm drawn to it. And nowhere could be more eerie than the area I lived in from age seven to eighteen, for it was London's East End, Jack the Ripper territory, where much was in ruins, demolished by bombs during the Second World War, and what remained had been neglected for so long that a general razing was considered to be the only solution to the blight. My street, or 'turning' as it was called in those days, was narrow – two good jumps could take you from pavement to pavement – and the top half was filled with gutted houses, dark-windowed shells whose interiors had been destroyed by direct hits from Hitler's bombers (Tyne Street was not far from the docks and on the doorstep of the City's square mile, both areas specified targets for the *Luftwaffe*). Many large rats lived in those ruined houses and it took some courage to walk by the open doorways on a dark and foggy night.

The road itself was cobble-stoned and the lighting was from feeble gas lamps mounted high on the walls (although we eventually 'went electric,' I can still remember the man with the long pole, who walked through the streets in the evening lighting the gas lights). Two doors away from my own home – this at the very bottom of the turning and facing up the street – was Old Castle Alley, a tiny alleyway cut through the buildings on either side and roofed by one of them, where Jack the Ripper allegedly fled after slicing one of his victims.

INTRODUCTION

Behind Tyne Street was Petticoat Lane, a street market to which half the population of London, it seemed, flocked on Sunday mornings. I was always fluid as I passed through those bustling crowds (I never walked, I always ran in those days), scouring the stalls for old comics or books, or going to the Catholic church at Moorfields about half a mile away. At 1p.m. precisely, something magical always happened: the people evaporated, the stalls disappeared, and the area became a ghost town, with only water lorries trundling through, flushing away the rubbish and making the streets shiny wet. From bedlam to tranquillity within the space of half-an-hour.

That unearthly transition has never lost its impact on me and it's a contrast I've used in more than one of my novels. In fact, deserted London has a deep fascination for me: witness *The Rats*, *The Fog*, *Domain*, *The Dark*. As a boy I cycled around the bomb-sites beneath the shadow of St Paul's Cathedral, those desolate, wide open spaces, now filled so tight with office complexes and skyscrapers, a private playground for my own war games. On weekends I claimed the docks and deserted canyons of the City's financial quarter for my own adventures, for in those days they were virtually people-less. Even the Tower of London became a backyard to me, despite its tourist hordes.

These places, then, played their part in my formative years; but none have influenced me more than the house in which I lived.

Number 26, Tyne Street, was a tall, narrow house, built probably around the turn of the century. Its crumbling brick walls contained three floors and a basement (an iron grid set in the pavement outside protected the below-ground cellar window), and at the back there was a ten-by-ten yard with toilet and coalshed; beyond its high wall was a longer yard, the dumping ground for the market stall-holders. The house's interior walls were made of wood, painted brown and cream, and the staircase that took you to the bedrooms above was almost spiral, so narrow were its turns. The wood creaked. It creaked with the cold, it creaked with the heat. It especially creaked in the middle of the night.

Now I spent many late nights alone in the house, drawing; I was always drawing pictures, sometimes painting. And more often than not the house would suddenly be plunged into utter darkness – the light meter, one of those old boxes you had to feed shillings into, seemed to need constant replenishment at night. Always without warning, without mercy. If I was lucky I'd find a shilling on the mantel; and if I was lucky again I'd find a box of matches to light my way down to the *cellar*. Yes, of all places, the electricity meter was down in the cellar.

We've all had our nightmares, but this was a real and regular one for a ten-year-old kid. I still wince at the memory: the feeling my way along painted wooden

The Pool of London: the banks of the Thames, particularly beside the Tower of London, became the kids' seaside beaches.

The bomb-sites around St Paul's Cathedral: in the 1950s· they were my adventure playground.

Petticoat Lane: my treasure trove of second-hand comics, books and records.

walls, the first set of steps at the end of the short corridor, the big black bolted back door that guarded us from whatever crept around the yard at night, the turn into the next set of steps that led to the cellar itself.

Two ways to go at the bottom of the stairs, for the meter was housed behind a wood partition, a strange divide to that basement that I never quite understood: straight ahead through a hole in the partition (which meant clambering over coal that hadn't been stored outside), or deeper into the cellar itself, past the divider, then turn right to reach the coin box. Some choice. The first – but shorter – way meant getting black with coal, the second meant clambering over odd junk: broken furniture, wheel-less bikes, orange boxes waiting to be chopped up for fire-wood, an old washing mangle, a copper used for boiling beetroot to be sold on my father's market stall. The speedy way was through the hole, but the decision was usually made on whether or not I had a match.

Often sightless, I'd locate the box, imagining all manner of creatures down there in the dark with me, then feel for the coin slot. In with the shilling, a quick, sharp twist of the small protruding lever (I always thought of *The Monkey's Paw* at this point, an X-rated movie I somehow happened to see at the tender age of *six*; a distraught mother wants her dead son back from the grave and the withered, dismembered and mummified monkey's paw gives her wrist a quick painful twist before granting her wish). The light in the corridor upstairs would come on – unfortunately the one in the cellar had a broken switch and had never worked – and although utter darkness retreated, other impenetrable shadows were formed. So if certain things seemed to move down there in the inky blackness it was only my own skinny little body reflecting the faint light from above, and if there were sounds behind me as I fled, well, probably my haste had disturbed some unsteady junk or perhaps startled small creatures that enjoyed this gloomy sub-world.

Little wonder then, you might think, that tales of darkness and terror eventually became a large part of my life.

But the main point is that these places – this old creepy house, the deserted streets of London, gutted buildings alive with rats, devastated sites, even churches wherein the 'supernatural' dwelt – were the initial 'locations' of my life, the ones that had an impact on me and left their imprint where imagination feeds off memories. And always I've sought more, looking well beyond my own environs, searching for places that will trigger off something in my thoughts, spark off ideas, make me shudder, fill me with foreboding. Even scare me silly.

I'll tell you about a few of them...

BURIAL PLACES

I was an art student at the beginning of the 1960s and although my course was graphic design, photography and print, I spent one day a week, along with fellow students, sketching outdoors. Stations, canals, museums, markets – locations were anywhere with interesting architecture, artefacts, or an abundance of life. But the most popular place with me was where there was an abundance of death: Highgate Cemetery, London.

It was there that the imagination – if it had a particularly macabre bent – could run riot. The graves and tombs were overgrown with foliage, grass and weeds, but the elaborate Victorian excesses could still be appreciated, the mutilated angels and stained crosses could still be wondered at. As I sat there with pad, pencils and brushes, I'd imagine movement in the soil, the muffled beating of a heart from a body long since rotted coming to my ears through the earth, the raspy whisper of a voice not used to conversing with the living... Darkly-halcyon days.

Especially inspiring (again, if your imagination leaned towards the macabre – and mine did) was the Egyptian Avenue, a dusky canyon built into the hillside and entered through a huge arch flanked by sinister obelisks. I must admit to a kind of Hammer-House-of-Horror thrill as I walked past the heavy metal doors set into its dark walls, each one of these guarding individual vaults containing shelves of deteriorating coffins. More often than not a fellow student lurked in the doorway waiting to emerge, arms outstretched, legs stiff with rigor mortis, tongue lolling

from open mouth and eyes big and staring. Spooky the first time, monotonous around the seventh.

Just as daunting were the Terrace Catacombs, a great menacing gallery filled with over eight hundred coffin recesses, a virtual City of the Dead in itself. No wonder Highgate Cemetery was, and still is to this day, a popular meeting place for satanists, wannabe vampires and necrophiliacs.

In my earlier years, my older brother and I used to take a short cut on our way home from the cinema in Commercial Road, Poplar. It was a winding dirt track through an old bombed-out churchyard. A screen of trees, foliage and a battered stone wall hid the blasted tombs and graves from the main road and all that remained of the church itself was the gutted shell of its tower. More often than not we would pass through those ruins at dusk or late-evening and there was one point midway that provided a special thrill. Two paces away from the track stood a large tomb whose heavy stone lid had been blown slightly askew, leaving a dark – oh so very dark – hole at one corner.

This was the hard part for us and our hearts always raced in anticipation of what we had to do. The anticipation was not necessarily unpleasant. With a quick breath we'd scoot past 'that hole in the tomb', our imaginations shrieking at the thought of skeletal hands, pieces of corrupted flesh falling from bony fingers, reaching out from those black depths to grab us as we sped by. Five yards clear and air would escape our lungs in a great *whoop* as if we'd broken surface after some perilous dive.

The thing of it is, we could have just as easily skirted that old churchyard and stuck to the busy pavements around it, adding no more than a minute or so to our journey. But we didn't choose to. For without the thrill, the scare, the bowel-clenching moment of ultimate terror, the walk home from the cinema would have been precisely that: a walk home from the cinema, with no excitement, no test of valour; pretty boring in fact.

Sometimes I even went through that desecrated graveyard on my own.

On reflection, this might well have been the time when the incongruity (although at that tender age the word was not in my vocabulary) of the location first struck me: the quiet if sinister burial ground where (thankfully) nothing stirred, against the clamour of the busy Whitechapel Road, just greenery and a broken wall the dividing line. It was certainly a place that stayed in my mind, for many years later I was to use it in my first novel. You see, late at night old dossers – tramps whose main sustenance was methylated spirits – gathered there around wood fires to socialise and sleep. They and Mary Kelly, the subject of my story's excursive vignette (a bag-lady whose rapid descent to squalor and degradation was caused by an almost religious sexual goal), met their terrible fate at the hands – no, at the *teeth* – of a particularly nasty breed of *Rattus rattus*.

Since those early days, and in my role as writer, I've dropped by many a burial place. Indeed, in my location researches I inevitably make a point of browsing through the local graveyard. And although not addicted to them (God forbid!) I am attracted to their loneliness. Strangely, to me it seems that it's the presence of the dead rather than the absence of the living that pervades the atmosphere. Can the dead be lonely? Of course not.

Yet it's the very bleakness of such situations that I seek in every location I visit. And burial places never let me down.

GATHERINGS FROM GRAVEYARDS

The first London cemetery on modern lines was that at Kensal Green, established in 1832, but it was still far from the norm in 1839 when the surgeon George Walker visited 50 graveyards and wrote a scathing attack on the filthy practices he discovered. Entitled *Gatherings from Graveyards Particularly those of London, with a concise History of the Modes of Interment amongst Nations from earliest periods and a Detail of Dangerous and fatal Results produced by the unwise and revolting custom of Inhuming the Dead in the Midst of the Living,* it contained sick-making revelations.

A frequent complaint was the presence of rotting human flesh close to, or even on, the very surface of these places. In one instance, a London woman noticed amongst a heap of graveyard rubbish the finger of her own mother who had been buried there not long before.

Cases of drunken grave diggers were frequent, as were sales of newly dug-up coffins on the second-hand market. 'Coffin Furniture', the expensive metal fittings adorning the woodwork, found eager parsimonious purchasers with an eye for a bargain. Even the contents of coffins could be made to turn a profit, as human bones were ground down to make manure. Walker reported an episode that occurred in the precincts of Globe Fields Chapel, Mile End, of a lad caught leaving the cemetery with one bag of coffin nails and another of bones, both of which he intended to sell.

Adding weight to his findings, Walker also cited a contemporary newspaper report castigating the St Giles's Burial Ground, not far from Charing Cross Road:

'What a horrid place is St Giles's church yard! It is full of coffins, up to the surface. Coffins are broken up before they are decayed, and bodies removed to the "bone house" before they are sufficiently decayed to make their removal decent...Here in the place of "Christian burial", you may see human heads covered with hair; and here, in this "consecrated ground", are human bones with flesh still adhering to them...'

Bad enough, you'd think. But Walker – strong-stomached – found worse:

'In making a grave a body, partly decomposed, was dug up, and placed on the surface at the side, slightly covered with earth; a mourner stepped on it, the loosened skin peeled off, he slipped forward, and had nearly fallen into the open grave.'

Then there was the appearance, at the Dissenters' Enon Chapel, Clement's Lane, of huge numbers of thin, fly-like insects which crawled out of occupied coffins. Said coffins were stored below the chapel used as a children's Sunday School, and as only a flimsy wooden floor separated the school from the cellar, the building was often filled during classes with swarms of humming black insects which the children called 'body bugs'.

On another occasion a tradesman was called in to build a drain in a house adjoining the

Russell Court Burial Ground, near Drury Lane: he took up the floor of the building only to find large quantities of human bones. 'It was supposed that they had been dragged thither by rats, vast numbers of which annoy the inhabitants in the proximity of the burial ground,' wrote Walker.

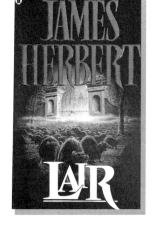

The vicar entered the covered gateway to the church and paused to gaze up at the ancient building's steeple. It wasn't high, the pinnacle barely topping the highest branches of the surrounding trees, yet it reached upwards in solid defiance of its earthly base as though it could pierce the heavens themselves, and feed through its funnel shape the souls of the faithful. Its spiritual brashness gave his heart a sudden uplift. Doubts were a part of serving, for if there were none there would be no searching for answers, no obstacles to surmount – no tests to be judged by. This was his time of testing and when it was through he would have a sturdier faith, a stronger belief in God.

The little church always gave him this sudden surge of optimism, which was why he often visited it so early in the morning. The negative thoughts of the night had to be swiftly allayed if he was to survive the day, and a quiet hour at the altar helped him build his barrier. His feet crunched along the narrow gravel path running between the gravestones towards the church porch, his eyes avoiding the slabs of grey on either side, and it was only when his hand was on the circular metal handle of the door that he heard the scrabbling sounds that came from the rear of the building.

He slowly turned his head in that direction, a curious coldness stiffening his spine. Listening intently, he tried to place the sound. It was as if earth was being scattered, the sound of someone or *something* digging. It would have to be an animal of some kind, for he could not recognise the familiar thud of a spade biting into the earth, nor the dull clump as the tossed soil struck the ground in one loose lump. This was a ceaseless barrage of scattered dirt.

The splintering of wood made him jump.

Dread rising in him, he left the porch and continued on down the path, his footsteps loud, wanting to warn whatever was behind the church of his approach, wanting the area to be deserted before he reached it.

'Who's there?' he called out and for a moment, there was silence. Then the scrabbling noise began again.

The vicar reached the corner of the church, the ground beside the path dropping away to a lower level, stone steps leading down to the grass-covered graveyard. From there he could see the freshly opened grave.

It was the plot in which old Mrs Wilkinson had been laid to rest the day before, untidy piles of earth lying in scattered heaps around the rough, circular hole. The gnawing of wood told him the worst.

Rage made him tear down the steps. What animal would burrow into the earth for the flesh of a human corpse? He reached the edge of the hole and cried out at the sight below.

READING ABBEY, BERKSHIRE

If a mediaeval monarch died far from home, a practical problem arose: how to preserve the body to avoid decomposition on the long arduous journey back for burial. The most perishable organs – eyes, brain, heart and intestines – were speedily removed, preferably by someone with due learning and status such as a doctor or a monk, but in emergencies, cooks or butchers – anyone who knew about cutting meat – were dragged in to perform the operation. The rest of the corpse would be soaked in a preservative – normally wine or vinegar – and strongly pungent aromatics, for reasons that would become distressingly obvious if the royal pickling failed to work. Finally the body would be sewn into a container made of tough hides. It didn't always succeed: the ineffective preservation of King Henry I of England led to emetic experiences for those coming into contact with the reeking royal carrion.

Henry died in his castle of Lions in northern France on 1 December 1135, and was the next day taken to the church of Our Lady in Rouen. There, on the evening of the second, his body was opened up and his bowels, tongue, heart, eyes and brain were buried in Rouen. The rest was roughly embalmed and taken to Caen in Normandy to wait for a suitable day to cross the Channel to England. The embalming was only partially successful. Apparently the physician who excised the decaying viscera died of toxaemia, and chronicler Henry of Huntingdon revelled in the opportunity to pontificate: 'Observe...to what horrible decay, to what a loathsome state his body was reduced! Mark how things end and learn to despise what so perishes and comes to nothing.' Henry's remains ended up waiting for weeks, getting higher all the time. Finally the royal corpse set sail after Christmas and was eventually laid to rest in the now vanished royal abbey of Reading.

The mourners were grouped around the open grave, dark clothes struck grey by the sunlight. Stained white crosses, slabs, and smiling cracked angels were dispassionate observers in the field of sunken bones. The mushy cadence of traffic could be heard in the distance; somewhere a radio was snapped off, the graveyard worker realising a ceremony was in progress. The priest's voice carried as a muffled intonation to the low knoll where the figure waited in the yew's shadow.

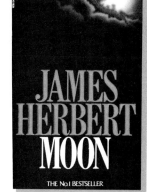

When the tiny coffin was lowered, a woman staggered forward as if to forbid the final violation of her dead child. A man at her side held the woman firm, supporting her weight as she sagged. Others in the group bowed their heads or looked away, the mother's agony as unbearable as the untimely death itself. Hands were raised to faces, tissues dampened against cheeks. The features of the men were frozen, pale plastic moulds.

It watched from the hiding place and smiled secretly.

The little casket disappeared from view, swallowed by the dank soil, green-edged lips eagerly wide. The father threw something in after the coffin, a bright-coloured object – a toy, a doll, something that had once been precious to the child – before earth was scattered into the grave.

Reluctantly, yet with private relief, the bereaved group began to drift away. The mother had to be gently led, supported between two others, her head constantly turning as if the dead infant were calling her back, pleading with her not to leave it there, lonely and cold and corrupting. The grief overwhelmed and the mother had to be half-carried to the waiting funeral cars.

The figure beneath the tree stayed while the grave was filled.

To return again later that night.

MILDENHALL, SUFFOLK

To the south of the church, surrounded by later graves, is a rare example of a mediaeval charnel house – you can see it covered in ivy here – a building in which unearthed bones and fragments of bodies (not always fully decomposed) from previous burials were piled up, waiting for reinterment. The charnel house was more often the crypt of the church, which sometimes gave rise (literally) to the disgusting stench of decomposition during services. The Mildenhall example, mistakenly called the Read Memorial, was endowed in 1387 and still has the remains of a chapel to St Michael over it. Charnel houses were once widespread, and they were disturbing places: the seventeenth-century writer John Aubrey wrote that the largest charnel house he ever saw was at Hereford Cathedral, and that a poor woman lived in it, using its bones to fuel her fire. But what did she use for food?

The cemetery. The girl must have been visiting it with her mother when she'd wandered off. She must have had a dead relative – her father, perhaps? – buried here. Now where's she got to? There doesn't seem to be anyone else around; her mother's probably gone off looking for her. Then he saw a flash of pale blue and he caught sight of her dashing between old, grey headstones. She stopped and looked back at him, standing perfectly still as though waiting for him to move. When he didn't, she raised an arm in a beckoning motion. With a resigned sigh, he walked up the gravelly path between the graves towards her.

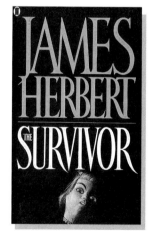

'Wait a minute,' he called out, 'I don't think your mother's here!' But she ran on again.

He saw the vast, freshly dug area and wondered at it. There appeared to be over a couple of hundred mounds of dark earth, obviously outlining fairly new graves, and then he realised what they signified. This was the mass grave for the victims of the air crash! Ugh, how horrible, he thought. The poor little thing must have lost someone in the disaster. He noticed the clear centre area where the large tombstone bearing all the names of the dead would be eventually placed. The boys in his house had frightened each other with their macabre stories of how all the bodies were mixed up and nobody could be sure that the right limbs and heads were buried with the right torsos. He shuddered violently and felt goose pimples rise on his flesh.

HEREFORD CATHEDRAL

Perhaps because preserving bodies in vinegar sometimes failed, the Middle Ages tried another method – boiling down cadavers in wine or water till the flesh left the bones. The resultant clean skeleton could be transported long distances whilst any fleshy residue could be given local burial. This was the case when Thomas de Cantilupe, Bishop of Hereford, died in Tuscany, Italy in 1282. His flesh was buried in the church of St Severus near Florence, but his bones were returned to England and initially placed in the Lady Chapel of Hereford Cathedral.

WORCESTER CATHEDRAL

In the eighteenth century, frank curiosity and disrespect lead to exceptional violations of long-buried remains – and being a royal corpse was no protection. When the tomb of King John in Worcester Cathedral was opened, a Mr Thompson of the town is supposed to have baited his hook with part of the decayed king, and carried the fish he caught with it 'in vulgar and brutal triumph through the streets'.

And, according to indignant historian C.H. Hale, writing in the early nineteenth century, worse happened to the remains of King Henry VIII's last Queen, Catherine Parr. Her tomb at Sudeley in Gloucestershire was broken into in 1782, 1784, 1786 and 1792. In the last episode 'the remains were exhumed by a band of Bacchanalians, at which time the outrages were so disgraceful that a veil must be drawn over them'. Nonetheless it was 'reported of the Bacchanalians concerned in the shameful scenes...that not one of them escaped an untimely death, all being snatched from existence with awful and appalling suddenness, which fact is still in the remembrance of some aged people yet living...'

DANBURY, ESSEX

The following episode apparently took place here in 1779. Inside a casing enclosed in an elm coffin, which was itself enclosed in a lead one and buried under a large stone, was discovered a body in a remarkable state of preservation. The explanation? It had been lying in a sort of slurry which observers thought looked like a ketchup made from mushrooms. One witness later wrote in an issue of The Gentleman's Magazine: *'As I never possessed the sense of smelling, and was willing to ascertain the flavour of the liquor, I tasted it.' He found it 'aromatic, though not very pungent, partaking of the taste of catsup and the pickle of Spanish olives'.*

BOUGHTON, NORTHAMPTONSHIRE

A very individual ghost makes Boughton graveyard a place to be wary of – an amorous spirit which changes gender as opportunity dictates. Seeing a pretty woman, it confronts her in the form of a handsome man, demands a kiss and then vanishes. Young men meet it as a lovely girl, equally eager for attention and equally elusive. It's thought this enterprisingly flirtatious spirit is a rare example of two souls combining in one manifestation. In Victorian times a newly married man died a mere three hours after his wedding ceremony, whereupon his distraught bride killed herself. Their joint phantom will haunt the church and its surroundings with no hope of release from heartache...

WEST DRAYTON, MIDDLESEX

A huge black bird is alleged to wheel round in the church and outside it and on one occasion it was seen to hit its wing and fall suddenly – unusually naturalistic behaviour for a supernatural creature – but no trace of it could then be found on the ground. A gruesome local explanation has the bird as the restless spirit of an unknown murderer who was mistakenly buried in consecrated ground, instead of in a lime pit in the local prison or, better, at nearby Harmondsworth Cross with a stake through his heart to prevent any vengeful ghostly manifestations.

PREMATURE BURIAL

Many of our private fears of interment derive from a deep-rooted terror of premature burial. In the past, there was good reason to dread such a fate.

Many criminals were hanged sufficiently to extinguish signs of life, but not life itself – in the Middle Ages, hanging was a form of slow strangulation rather than the neck-snapping drop of later centuries. It was customary for the family of the executed criminal to receive the body, and it was not unknown for the corpse suddenly to revive; such survivors usually received a royal pardon. John Evelyn's *Diary* from the seventeenth century tells of a celebrated case of a woman, executed for theft, who was subsequently revived and who would otherwise have been buried alive.

A number of medical conditions – fits, comas and so on – approximated the appearance of death in a temporary way and deceived the living with ghastly results, until the twentieth century. Victorian authors discussed the subject in depth, and newspapers ghoulishly reported incidents from all over the world. *Premature Burial and how it may be prevented,* by William Tebb and Colonel Edward Perry Vollum, published in 1896, described scores of nineteenth-century tragedies from Britain, Europe and the United States. Typical was the fate of George Hefdecker, a farmer from Pennsylvania, whose end was reported from *The Progressive Thinker* of 14 November 1891. The farmer died, it seemed, of a heart failure, and was temporarily buried in a neighbour's cemetery plot while his family purchased one for him. This was available a few days later, but... 'When the casket was opened at the request of his family, a horrifying spectacle was presented. The body had turned round, and the face and interior of the casket bore the traces of a terrible struggle with death in its most awful shape. The distorted and bloodcovered features bore evidence of the agony endured. The clothing about the head and neck had been torn into shreds, as was likewise the lining of the coffin. Bloody marks of finger nails on the face, throat and neck, told of the awful despair of the doomed man, who tore his own flesh in his terrible anguish. Several fingers had been entirely bitten off, and the hands torn with the teeth until they scarcely resembled those of a human being.'

To fear such an end was far from irrational – in 1895, it was calculated that at least 2,700 people in England and Wales were buried alive each year. Visitors to the French port of Bordeaux could see the results of such suffering for themselves. Excavations near the cathedral there had revealed a strip of burial ground which seemed to have unusual preserving qualities, as the bodies unearthed showed almost no signs of decay. Of around two hundred so discovered, thirty were displayed on iron frames in the cathedral, two of them showing hideously convincing signs of having undergone the prolonged agonies of premature burial. One had drawn its legs up to its stomach as though it had tried to use them to force its way out of the coffin; 'The look of horror remaining on its face was simply indescribable,' wrote a London doctor who saw it in 1870. The other had been found face down, its arms extended above the head as though trying to push out the roof of its last resting place.

Not surprisingly, many people went to extremes to avoid that fate, such as a Kent woman who early this century decreed in her will that on her death 'my body shall be stabbed to the heart to make sure that life is extinct'. Similarly Lady Burton, widow of Sir Richard Burton the writer on anthropology, left instructions that her heart should be pierced with a needle: she had a history of trances and was terrified that one of her attacks would be mistaken for death.

Other cases are so bizarre that they almost have a comic side to them. Take one particular lady, who was eventually buried in Rye churchyard in Sussex. Her tombstone, now gone, was said to show her sitting upright in her coffin. The story goes that she suffered from syncope, a kind of short-term loss of consciousness, and during one attack was pronounced dead. Her cadaver was wrapped in a shroud and taken to a local inn, where it was placed in a coffin to await interment the next day. When the inn's oven was lit to cope with the culinary requirements of a good wake, she revived and walked downstairs to warm herself by the fire, complaining to an almost insensible cook of the cold. She subsequently lived for several years before death unequivocally claimed her.

BASINGSTOKE, HAMPSHIRE

From The Uncertainty of the Signs of Death *by Surgeon M. Cooper, London, 1746:*

'At Basingstoke, in Hampshire, not many years ago, a gentlewoman of character and fortune was taken ill, and, to all appearance, died, while her husband was on a journey to London. A messenger was forthwith despatched to the gentleman, who returned immediately, and ordered everything for her decent interment. Accordingly, on the third day after her supposed decease, she was buried in the Holy Ghost Chapel, at the outside of the town, in a vault belonging to the family, over which there is a school for poor children, endowed by a charitable gentleman in the reign of Edward VI. It happened the next day that the boys, while they were at play, heard a noise in the vault, and one of them ran and told his master, who, not crediting what he said, gave him a box on the ear and sent him about his business; but, upon the other boys coming with the same story, his curiosity was awakened, so that he sent immediately for the sexton, and opened the vault and the lady's coffin, where they found her just expiring. All possible means were used to recover her life, but to no purpose, for she, in her agony, had bit the nails off her fingers, and tore her face and head to that degree, that, notwithstanding all the care that was taken of her, she died in a few hours in inexpressible torment.'

HOLY
PLACES

Churches have played a significant part in my life. I was brought up as a Roman Catholic and it was inside a church that I first learned of the supernatural. I was informed of the world of spirits, of saints, and of the one Supreme Being. I learned of the constant struggle between God and the Devil, of goodness against wickedness, and to me it seemed like an enthralling struggle. Little wonder then, that years later the consistent theme of most of my novels became the conflict between Good and Evil.

Strangely though, churches are lonely places for me, places in which to meditate, to examine one's own self, rather than be brought together with others in celebration. The Mass is there as a glorious ceremony, a ritual of unification as well as deification, yet I'm never more aware of my own singularity (in the modest sense) than when I'm among a happily joined congregation of worshippers. The aloneness of the individual is emphasised rather than overcome at such times, which is an odd effect given the worthy intentions of the religious service itself.

The plus side of this for me is that for my role as writer and observer churches provide wonderfully austere and, when dealing with the more gothic examples, sinister focal points.

In 1982 I found a location that provided three visual elements that inspired a story of miracles in the high-tech era of consumerism and cynicism. These were: an ancient church; a cemetery; a dying, grotesquely twisted and gnarled oak tree. To these I added a fourth component: a young innocent girl. I was told that the last two witches to be burned at the stake in England had been found hiding in this particular Sussex church, which confirmed to me that this would be an ideal setting for a tale of religion and witchcraft in the modern age. That real church and oak opened this chapter: and the graveyard, plus another actual location essential to the story – the exterior and interior of a smaller, lonelier church near a dour Tudor manor house – follow on the next few pages.

The story was called *Shrine* and one of the fascinations for me, and which became part of the subtext, was the stability of this ancient building – and institution, of course – whilst the world outside was changing at an ever-accelerating pace. Those same ceremonies performed basically in the same way, year after year, century after century – the Mass itself, the marriages, the christenings, the funerals, the Benedictions, the confessions – and all they represented, must have become ingrained in the very atmosphere of the church, in the walls themselves; yet outside, culture and society had altered fantastically (certainly no more witches being burnt) and materialism had become a new kind of God. The growing discord between ancient beliefs and practices and the mutable twentieth century (and soon the twenty-first century) had created a *frisson* that appealed to me as a subject for examination and in a small way, *Shrine* was an attempt to do just that.

One church I visited in the county of Berkshire evoked powerful ideas of hauntings and played a pervasive part in an early novel. A year or so later after the book's publication I heard that the church was deemed 'haunted by demons' by its own vicar, who urged his bishops to order its closure. Naturally this intrigued me and I couldn't help wonder if these same weird occurrences – blood smeared on the walls and altar, drapes set on fire, statues overturned – in my book could have inspired some local malefactors to carry out such vandalism. However in the national newspapers the vicar insisted that the sacrilege was performed by evil spirits. It made a good story, and a particularly interesting one to me, but a few years later I discussed the affair with a 'ghost hunter' who was helping me with my researches for another novel and it was he who told me the full story of that specific 'haunting'. It seemed that the vicar's wife had become a little too 'compassionate' towards a number of his male parishioners; so much so, in fact, that her indiscretions had become the talk of the community and had driven the vicar to a nervous breakdown. The 'ghost hunter', who had been asked to investigate the matter, discovered that the vicar had manufactured the 'hauntings' and the desecrations himself in order to be moved on to another parish where he and his wife hopefully could start afresh. Whether or not my book had given him the idea for such mischief (I understand the novel was particularly popular in the area) I'll never know, but it was an odd example of life following fiction, and perhaps a lesson to the more gullible ghost seeker that all such events should be examined with an impartial and even pragmatic attitude. And perhaps that all holy places should be revered by their clergy as much as they are by atmosphere-hungry authors.

Something tripped her – probably the corner of a flattened gravestone – and she tumbled forward, her knees smearing green and brown from the soft earth. She cried out, but there was no sound, and quickly regained her feet, eager to reach the wall and not knowing why. She kept to the narrow path leading through the cluttered graveyard and stopped only when she had reached the wall. Alice peered over, the highest stone on a level with her chest. The pregnant sheep were no longer munching grass; all heads were raised and looking in the same direction.

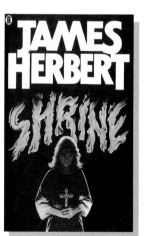

They did not move even when Alice clambered over the wall and ran among them.

Her footsteps slowed, her shoes and socks soaked by the long grass. She seemed confused and swivelled her head from left to right. Her small hands were clenched tight.

She looked directly ahead once more and the half-smile returned, gradually broadening until her face showed only rapturous wonder.

A solitary tree stood in the centre of the field, an oak, centuries old, its body thick and gnarled, its stout lower branches sweeping outwards, their furthest points striving to touch the ground again. Alice walked towards the tree, her steps slow but not hesitant, and fell to her knees when she was ten yards away.

. . . .

The tree was just a tree. A tired old oak. A silent witness to passing time. He could see the sheep grazing in a far corner of the field, their bodies yellowy-grey and bloated, concerned only for the next mouthful of grass and the growing heaviness in their pregnant bellies...

The tree was withered; the years had made it a twisted thing. It dominated that part of the field, a gargantuan guardian, innumerable arms thrown outwards to warn off intruders. A grotesque shape disrobed of summer leaves, intimidating in its ugliness. Yet, he told himself, it was just a centuries-old oak, its lower branches bowed, bark scarred and dry, its vitality patiently stolen by time. But why did the girl kneel before it?

. . . .

She pushed the door open wider and stepped in from the porch. The light inside was dull, diffused by the thick, leaded windows.

The door made a low growling noise as she closed it, a muffled thump disturbing the stillness inside when it shut completely. Nancy looked around the miniature church, loving its quaintness, impressed by its tradition. A leaden font stood before her, the dark, letter-ornamented metal speaking of another time, a different era. Nearly all the pews were boxed in, the panels chest-height, narrow doors allowing entry. Whole families probably sat in each one, Nancy assumed, cut off from their neighbours, enclosed in their own small islands of worship. The wood panelling was stripped of any varnish, its bareness somehow

complementing the character of the chapel itself. No more than thirty to forty feet away, at the head of the narrow aisle, was the tiny altar.

. . . .

A long, straight path led from the carpark to the mediaeval church; to the right, about a quarter of a mile away, stood the daunting manor house, an impressive structure of Tudor design, yet curiously empty-looking, lifeless. Indeed, it probably was at that time, for Fenn had learned earlier that the owner had died some years before and his family only stayed in the house for certain months of the year, preferring sunnier climes in the winter months.

As he trod the narrow path, the church loomed up like an image framed in a slow-moving zoom lens, and he began to feel very lonely and very isolated. Like the manor house in the distance, St Peter's was constructed of grey stone, green-stained with age; one section of the roof was covered with large moss-covered slates, the rest with red tiles; the windows were leaded, the glass thick and smoothly rippled as though each pane had been placed in its frame still hot and melting. He saw now how oddly-shaped the building was and could imagine the various segments being added at various times through the centuries, each portion reflecting its own period. The path led past the church, presumably to where the entrance had to be, for he could see no doors as he approached. The expanse he had just crossed had been bare; now there were trees, mostly oak, around the church, and the wind

rustled through the empty branches, an urgent, rushing sound that increased his sense of isolation. Small branches broke away and scuttled in the air before reaching the earth; stouter branches lay scattered, victims of previous, stronger gusts, resembling twisted human limbs. The horizon, just above the distant Downs, now glowed silver in a strip that was held level by the dark, laden clouds above. The contrast between broody clouds and condensed sky was startling.

Fenn stepped off the path into rough grass to get near one of the church windows and, cupping a hand between brow and glass, peered in. There was an unappealing gloom inside and he could just make out the empty pews enclosed by wood panelling. At first glance it reminded him of a holy cattleshed. He took his hand away and twisted his neck, nose almost pressed against the glass, in an effort to see more. There were other windows opposite that threw little light into the interior, but he could just make out the shape of a font and more enclosed benches nearby. A movement caught his eye and it was so sudden that he drew back a few inches. Then he realised, the blood vessels in his throat seeming to constrict, that the action was not inside the church, but was a reflection in the glass.

He turned quickly and saw there was nothing there. Just a swaying branch.

Creepy, he told himself. Creepy, creepy, creepy.

Hoisting the hold-all back onto his shoulder, he rejoined the path and headed for the front of the church. When he reached the corner the wind tore into him with fresh force, driving the rain into his face like ice pellets. A square tower rose above him, too short and stubby to be majestic, reaching no more than forty feet into the air, its rampart top almost as grey as the clouds above it. A matt, rust-coloured door stood beneath the tower, the shade drab and unimaginative, paying no dues to the history it guarded.

. . . .

The roof groaned loudly as the wind pounded on it; something broke away, probably a slate, and slid down, its fall muffled by the soft earth around the church. Fenn looked up anxiously and assured himself that the church had stood up to such battering for centuries and was unlikely to collapse around him now. Nevertheless, he quickly opened the hold-all and put the three vellum-covered documents inside, first placing the loose leaves in the back of the book they had fallen from.

The church door was rattling insanely and nothing could be seen through the windows, so fierce was the rain. He began stuffing the other books, sheets and vestments back into the chest, unwilling to search any further, the urge to be away from the church too great. He had the same sense of black oppression that he'd experienced in the crypt of St Joseph's. The lid closed with a heavy thump and Fenn stood, relieved that it was done. Back to the car now, away from this godawful place, with its tearing wind and dark, dark church ... He hadn't noticed before just how dark it had become.

He stepped into the aisle, averting his eyes from the altar. The howling wind outside sounded like the wailing of lost souls. The door before him shook violently and something made him back away. The lift bar above the lock jiggled up and down as if some neurotic hand outside were playing with it. The wood trembled within its frame and he could sense the pressure behind it, the gale screeching for entry.

SUDBURY CHURCH, SUFFOLK

It looks innocuous, doesn't it: the typical proud church in a quiet country town. The sort of place to visit before having a cream tea. But like so many places, this has another, darker side in its past. St Gregory's is the mother church of ancient Sudbury, one of three mediaeval parishes in the town. The building, almost entirely Perpendicular architecture of the fourteenth and fifteenth centuries, was largely the creation of Simon Sudbury, Archbishop of Canterbury from 1375 to 1381; and he gives Sudbury its ghostly history. The Archbishop chose the wrong side in contemporary politics, when the consequences were more than just losing one's seat – Sudbury was beheaded by the forces of Wat Tyler during the Peasants' Revolt. His decapitated body lies in the choir aisle of Canterbury Cathedral, many miles to the south, but his head is supposed to be buried in St Gregory's. Since many ghosts are reputed to walk in search of missing limbs, it is not surprising that an anxious Simon has been seen, searching the church for his head. But is the ghost headless?

MINSDEN CHAPEL, HERTFORDSHIRE

Not far from bustling Hitchin is a small roofless chapel, almost devoid of architectural features now, which has quite a ghostly past. Built in the fourteenth century and abandoned in Stuart times, Minsden Chapel is alive with phantom activity on All Hallows' Eve. It is said that horses and dogs sense a presence, while human visitors have attested to the appearance of a ghostly monk (which is odd – Minsden was never an abbey). More than one person has reported the ringing of the chapel's bells, followed by the sighting of a cowled form near the south arch of the building. He bows his head, then retreats up stairs which are no longer there, finally vanishing in silence, though the music has been known to come back after his disappearance.

Peter Underwood, in his book A Gazetteer of British Ghosts, *writes of the time he visited the place, and though he saw no monk, he did hear fleeting notes of inexplicable music, as did a friend with him – yet strangely, the third member of the party, the writer's brother, heard nothing at all.*

He passed through the opening to the lawns which housed their few important gravestones and surrounded the cathedral, his eyes constantly narrowed, peering into the murk, trying to make out the path that led to the very doors of the ancient place of worship. Where was the glow? Surely he should have come upon it by now? He would have to make a circuit of the building, they'd insisted the centre was in this particular area. It could have moved on, of course, but there was very little breeze to stir it.

But as he approached the cathedral's entrance, he noticed a faint half-glow.

He stopped dead. Was it possible? Was the nucleus, the heart of the disease, housed within the great church? Could it have drifted into Winchester Cathedral and become trapped inside its ancient but solid stone walls?

Another, more disturbing, thought jarred Holman's mind.

What if it hadn't drifted in by accident? Could it possibly be self-motivated? It was an incredible idea and he tried to dismiss it from his mind. It was too fantastic, too much like science-fiction. But then everything that had happened was too fantastic.

The thought persisted.

He walked on, a coldness creeping through his body, his steps noiseless and cautious. He tried to fight the chill that enveloped him, reassuring himself with the thought that the sinister circumstances, the loneliness and the lack of clear vision were all working together, attacking his imagination, allies to fear.

He saw that the glow – or was it just a brighter tone of yellow? – was definitely coming from the open doorway. Had he the nerve to confront its source lurking inside?

'Fuck it!' It was a soft spoken war cry. He went on.

Lingering at the entrance, he peered into the brighter mist. The air was much harder to breathe in, the acidity burnt his nostrils and throat. He reached for the oxygen mask looped over his shoulder and was about to remove the smog mask when something flickered in the corner of his vision. He froze and studied the spot in the fog from where the movement had come. Imagination again? He saw nothing, only the patterns made by the swirls of the mist. He listened and heard nothing but the imagined beating of his own heart.

Holman looked towards the source of the glow. It was at its strongest at the centre of the

cathedral's vast interior, near the altar. It seemed to have no definable shape, its outer edges constantly changing their line and only visible because of the sudden contrast in yellows: the apparently clear clean yellow of the nucleus itself, against the murkier, greyer yellow of its protective screen, the fog. It was impossible to tell the size of the strangely writhing shape, his vision was too impaired by the surrounding layers of fog, but its very existence seemed to exude a malignancy, a malevolent growth that was frightening, yet perversely fascinating.

CANEWDON CHURCH, ESSEX

St Nicholas's is an unusually grand church for its area, dominated by a sturdy unfussy tower of mid-grey ragstone, four stages high, erected in the fifteenth century. A structure of obvious power and stability, it has occult significance – as long as it stands, seven witches will reside locally. Records attest to the activities of one George Pickingill, who this century cannily obtained beer from farming neighbours by threatening to halt their machinery by occult interference. Other local legends tell of a female witch – in one version, she is headless and, when seen close to the church, has the ability to hurl people into the air, letting them come to earth in a ditch; another sighting had her lurking around the church and its graveyard wearing a bonnet. Her displeasure is thought to be revenge for her execution nearby, many years ago.

WALTHAM ABBEY, ESSEX

This high altar is a splendid piece of Victorian devotional art – so why should a menacing pale light appear in the church before it, filling those who see it with inexplicable dread? The Abbey certainly has a long history: founded in 1030, it was refounded in style by King Harold in 1060, six years before his death at the Battle of Hastings. Thereafter it had a chequered career, being hugely extended in the twelfth century, only to be three-quarters demolished at the Reformation in the sixteenth century. Records of the closure of the monastery do not record terrible tortures. Why then, the malevolent presence? As yet, we are left in unnerved ignorance...

The chapel itself was infinitely brighter because of the high stained-glass windows which allowed light from outside to enter the vast hall in a muted diffusion of colour. To Clemens, though, the chapel still presented a forbidding and gloomy interior, and if Greene had not been following so closely behind him, he would have turned and fled there and then. The three boys stared down into the depths of the high-roofed fan-vaulted chapel with its rows of beautifully carved dark wooden pews facing each other across the wide aisle, those at the rear bearing the inscriptions of wealthy or famous past Etonians. The impressive marble altar, backed by its exquisite tapestries, at the end of the Perpendicular architectured chapel, was barely visible to them and the fragmentary wall-paintings running along the first half of the chapel's length were just grey blurs of darker shapes.

All three failed to see the white-coated figure sitting in the dark at the back of a row of pews. But all three were aware of the dank coldness that seeped through to their bones.

. . . .

The coldness hit him as soon as he entered the ante-chapel. He felt as if he had suddenly plunged into a gigantic freezer. Hardly pausing, he rushed to the entrance of the main chapel, oblivious of the darkness, full of anger for anyone who would dare violate his beloved chapel.

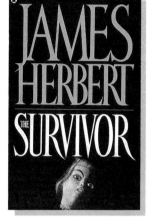

And there he stopped, unable to comprehend the sight before him.

It appeared that the vast hall was filled with dark, moving forms; forms that wavered and faded, undulating in a constantly changing mass, the eerie light from the enormous coloured windows confusing rather than accentuating the shapes. When he tried to concentrate on one figure, or a particular group of them, it seemed to disappear and form again after he had shifted his gaze. An overwhelming noise hit him, a bustling, howling sound, tumultuous in its overall effect. Listened to individually, however, the sounds were only whispers. Coarse and parched. Burnt voices.

In the dimness at the front of the chapel, before the altar, he could just make out a white-coated figure through the twisting throng. It seemed to be clutching two smaller bodies in a tight embrace. Fascinated, and horrified, the Head Master walked forward into the main chapel, the fascination drawing him in, the horror urging him to run away. He resisted the latter because he realised the figure in white held two boys in his arms – undoubtedly his pupils. His premonition of danger earlier that day had been correct; he did not understand what was happening, but he knew the boys – the College – were in mortal danger.

BATTLE ABBEY, SUSSEX
(OVERLEAF)

On 14 October 1066 took place one of the most ferocious and significant slaughters known to British history – the Battle of Hastings. The defeat of the Anglo-Saxon monarch Harold by the forces of William, Duke of Normandy was marked by the death of Harold himself, perhaps with an arrow in his eye as so graphically depicted in the Bayeux Tapestry. After the conflict, William vowed to thank God for the victory by founding an abbey on the site. By 1094 the church was ready to be consecrated, but nearly all William's abbey was, perhaps unwisely, destroyed at the Reformation by Sir Anthony Browne, who rapidly built a mansion in its place. At the first feast he gave there the spirit of a monk appeared, and announced to the horrified nobleman that his name would be removed from the land by means of fire and water. This came to pass when Cowdray Park, owned by Browne's descendant, was destroyed by fire in 1793, and in a short space of time the family was wiped out when the young Viscount was drowned in the Rhine.

As regards the Anglo-Saxon dead, a fountain of blood is said to spurt from the ground near the site of the altar, and after rain the vicinity seems to sweat blood – though this is probably due to chemicals in the local soil, which can have a reddish hue. Some visitors have reported seeing Harold himself, drenched in gore with an arrow gruesomely embedded in his face, staring with his one good eye over the scene of his defeat.

CANTERBURY CATHEDRAL

This is a moving and holy place, but has more than its fair share of gruesome connections. Archbishop Thomas Becket was murdered at the High Altar in 1187 by two knights loyal to the king. The martyrdom was vicious and bloody – legend has it that one soldier sliced off the top of Becket's skull as though it were a boiled egg and used the tip of his sword to prise out the brain like an oyster from its shell. Churchmen with an eye to the main chance scraped up as much of the Archbishop's remains as they could and made an infusion from them, while worshippers with strong stomachs mopped up his blood with their sleeves.
Still, it isn't just the site of Becket's murder that draws lovers of the hideous. The passage between the monk's infirmary and the pleasant-sounding Green Court is known as the

Dark Entry. Low, squat, dwarfed by the elegant vaults before it, and dating back to Norman times, it is eerily weathered and almost featureless. It's supposed to be haunted by Nell Cook, a servant of one of the Canons. Nell, besotted with her employer, discovered him in the act of seducing his own niece. With cunning refined by jealousy she prepared a game pie for them both, heavily laced with poison. They died in agony and Nell's reward was to be buried alive beneath the pavement of the Dark Entry. Her ghost is very vindictive – Friday nights are her favourite times to appear, and she could quite ruin the weekend, as to see her is to die.

DWELLING PLACES

Dwelling places have played a large part in many of my novels, from the swift-decaying mansion of *Haunted*'s Edbrook, to the mystical enchantment of Gramarye in *The Magic Cottage*. In fact, the very first line of my very first novel was: 'The old house had been empty for more than a year.' I went on to describe a lock-keeper's home I knew of that was by a canal in London's East End, and its subsequent desolate description set the mood for the whole piece, which was as much to do with the neglect of inner cities as it was with mutant rats on the rampage. One of my later creations, Neath in *Sepulchre*, was inspired by Tudor Compton Wynyates in Warwickshire – a fantasy pile of gables, turrets, towers and chimneys; it's captured in the next three photographs.

These old buildings, usually decrepit, always sinister, exist in a special reserve in my imagination, a place of eerie, cobwebbed interiors and grim edifices, their origins a combination of locations I've visited, my own humble childhood abode (as creepy as anything you'll find in my stories), and in film-sets that have entertained me for many, many years.

Who can forget the unease we felt when Hitchcock first showed us poor Norman Bates's psycho mother's house on the hill? Or the house in which four ghost hunters spent several hysterical nights together for Robert Wise's *The Haunting* (freely adapted in 1963 from Shirley Jackson's novel *The Haunting Of Hill House*), where massive oak doors bulged inwards as maleficent spirits outside strained to enter and footsteps pounded along dark, empty corridors? Then there was the mansion in which governess Deborah Kerr witnessed the corruption of her two young charges by the iniquitous spirit of their degenerate and very dead manservant Quint. The film was *The Innocents* (1961) made by Jack Clayton and based on the novel *The Turn Of The Screw* by Henry James, and here even the conservatory, with its abundance of blooms and plants, became a focal point of evil.

A favourite one of mine is *The Old Dark House* (1932), directed by James Whale (of *Frankenstein* fame) adapted from J.B. Priestley's novel *Benighted* and starring Boris Karloff and Charles Laughton. I saw the re-run in the early 1950s – don't ask me how an eight-year-old kid got in to see such an X-rated movie – and the images of that delapidated old manor, with its sombrous, uncongenial interiors, heavy beams and creaky staircases, the storm outside beating at its solid stone walls and wailing through open doorways, have stayed with me till this day.

Such films, along with many others, show how bricks and mortar, timber and glass, tile and shingle – materials of the real world – can conspire to evoke dark atmospheres, how a twitch of a curtain, a movement of shadow, a scratching against wood, can conjure impending horror. Rising towers, gargoyles and ramparts, cobwebbed stairways, locked attics, all are elements that lend a brooding menace. Sometimes they are a backdrop, sometimes they are the key player.

They can often be the horror writer's greatest prop.

His attention was irresistibly drawn back to the building itself, which appeared to be a curious jumble of irregular shapes. Principally Tudor in period, various sections had apparently been added on during its history with no regard for symmetry. The two gables were of unequal height and pitch, and the twisted chimneys were scattered almost inconsequently over the various roofs. There were different levels of turrets and a wing had been built onto the far side that stood higher than any other part of the building. Yet the overall image was not unpleasing and much of that had to do with the rich colouring of its brickwork, for the walls fairly glowed in the sunlight, the aged stone mottled a warm red, that same redness even within the roof tiles; the gables were half-timbered and the many turrets fringed grey, serving to complement the ruddiness of the main walls.

Although the building as a whole was compact, Neath was nevertheless hugely impressive, its position alone, between the small hills and the lake, supplying its own special grandeur.

. . . .

From this level Neath resembled a small monastery, thought Halloran. Except that there was nothing godly about the place. The day had become overcast, clouds hanging low and dark over the Surrey hills, so that now the redness of Neath's stonework had become subdued, the floridity deepening to a tone that was like ... the notion disturbed him ... like dull, dried blood. The house *looked* silent, as though it could never contain voices, footsteps, life itself. It might resemble a monastery, but it was hard to imagine invocations inside those walls.

. . . .

There were dark places in Neath, corners, niches, which sunlight could never touch, rooms gloomed in permanent dusk, corridors where dust motes seemed to clog the air, halls where footsteps echoed in emptiness. Yet there were also areas of dazzling light, the sun bursting through leaded windows with a force intensified by thick glass; these were cleansing places, where Neath's dank chill could be scoured from the body, although only briefly as other rooms, other corridors, were entered, brightness left behind like some sealed core.

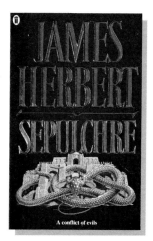

. . . .

He was before the lodge, a building of similar but darker stone to Neath itself, its grey-slated roof full of holes, windows dulled by grime. It looked unlived in. Yet someone inside had somehow allowed him to open the front gates (he'd had a better chance to examine the lock and still hadn't detected any electronic device installed within), for on first try the gates wouldn't budge. He studied the lodge a while longer before leaving the road and walking the short track up to the frontdoor. The best he got when he stretched a hand to the rusted bell was a dull clunk. He rapped on the wood.

There were no sounds from inside the house. No one came to open the door.

He knocked louder, then tried the handle; it was as though the door were solid to the stone itself, for it did not even jar in its frame. Halloran stepped back to look up at the first floor windows and saw nothing through the smeared glass. He walked back to the edge of the rutted road for a better view, but the angle merely rendered the windows an opaque black. He took one more backward step.

Halloran was suddenly cold, as if he'd stepped into a pocket of wintry air. He was being observed.

BREDE PLACE, SUSSEX

Folded into the wooded slopes of the Sussex countryside and almost hidden from the road,
Tudor Brede Place boasts a famous, grotesque legend that may be a shrewd invention. The
house was used by smugglers in Georgian times, so to keep away unwanted interference the
then owner described the activities of a predecessor, one of the Oxenbridge family. A giant,
he was alleged to have eaten local babies, and the young of the neighbourhood were only
saved when gangs of children captured him and cut him in half at the aptly named
Groaning Bridge nearby. Despite their actions, bits of the dismembered monster were
reputed to persist in the house, though how they were preserved is uncertain. Other more
straightforward ghosts are believed to occur here, including a priest and a headless man,
and monks were were seen during the Second World War, accompanied by the inexplicable
movement of objects.

WOODCROFT CASTLE, HUNTINGDONSHIRE

Started in the thirteenth century and added to over several centuries, this sturdy fortress has horrific associations. During the English Civil War the place was stoutly defended for the Royalists by Dr Michael Hudson, Chaplain to King Charles I, but despite his efforts the castle was taken by the Roundheads. It's said that as they swept through the castle the beseigers found Dr Hudson clinging to a gargoyle on the battlements. They hacked at his fingers with their pikes till they had amputated enough to make him lose his grip and fall into the moat below. Dazed and in terrible pain the stunned chaplain was then beheaded, despite earlier promises of mercy by the mendacious victors. Even death did not end his indignities. A shopkeeper from nearby Stamford cut out his tongue and sent it round the vicinity to be displayed as a grisly exhibit of Roundhead prowess.

Soon the car pulled into a driveway, the large, ornate gates at the entrance open wide, a long gravelled lane in some need of repair stretching ahead. The gardens on each side, after a brief expanse of woodland, were mainly laid to lawn, but the nearer the Wolseley drew to

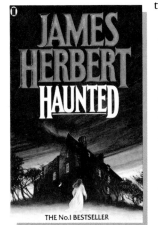

the house itself, the more elaborately landscaped they became. The flower beds, the trimmed hedges and shrubbery, had obviously been designed to present a variety of views, each one depending on how it was approached. The house reared from the gardens as though its architect had intended it to dominate rather than blend with the surrounds: Edbrook was imposing in its greyness and, despite swelling apses and well-ruled bay windows, somewhat disconcerting in its bleakness. Inexplicably, something seemed to lurch within Ash, an abrupt sagging of mood that left him strangely wearied. He peered up at the house and wondered at his own unease.

· · · · · · · · · ·

There was a coldness about Edbrook which only in part was to do with the shift in season. In certain rooms and corridors there was a dankness of air, in others a sense of emptiness that suggested they had not been used – nor, perhaps, even

entered – for some years. It was a large house though, and of a type Ash had investigated more than once before: it was not unusual for such homes (mainly due to inheritance taxes if the property was passed down through the family) to be frugally managed. It was not as though Edbrook had been neglected so much as that its upkeep appeared to be economically directed.

· · · · · · · · · ·

No lights, no glow from within. Edbrook was a vast black bulk that merged with the blackness of night clouds. A breeze stirred through the gardens, ruffling foliage, disturbing trees. In the woods, night creatures hunted, their skirmishes violent but brief. Honey fungus glowed blue-green on decaying tree trunks, beetles scuttled in the undergrowth. The moon was a pale ghost seen only behind slow-moving monoliths.

Inside the house, Ash slept; but he did not rest.

His dream was of water, a terrible churning pressure all around him. Occasionally his eyes would rise above its choppy surface and he would glimpse the riverbanks on either side, far out of reach and rushing away from him. He screamed and cold liquid filled his mouth; and that choking sensation was familiar to him.

· · · · · · · · · ·

He dressed slowly, without washing first – somehow the thought of cleansing himself never even entered his head. At the door he paused, hand resting on the handle. He waited there and wondered why he was reluctant to go out into the corridor. Ash realized that the very stillness of the house was unnerving him, for it seemed to hold a brooding quality, as though the timbers, the mortar, the house's *essence*, were waiting ... For what? He was annoyed at himself. David Ash, the ultimate pragmatist, was now indulging in fantasy, and a foolish one at that. Edbrook was just a house. No more than that. With a tragic history, to be sure, and one so strong that possibly it could still project its image long after the event. But that had little to do with haunting in the truest sense. There were no ghosts here, no spectres, nor spirits, to bother the living. Perhaps Edbrook entertained trickery though.

With that thought in mind, the investigator pulled open the door.

The corridor was empty, and he hadn't expected it to be otherwise. That was the eerie thing – the house itself felt empty. Empty of life. Yet still ... pensive.

Ash went along the dim corridor, passing the galleried stairway, glancing over into the well of the hallway as he did so. The very air inside Edbrook seemed heavy, aged. Perhaps the atmosphere had more to do with his own condition than actuality, for the previous night's trauma – *and* that of the first night – had left him weary and depressed. Even though he had slept most of the day away, there was a lassitude to his step and a muzziness inside his head that was difficult to dismiss.

. . . .

Yes, this was the place, for as she drew closer she could just discern the name EDBROOK etched into the brick pillars on either side of the drive. The gates were drawn back and she pulled off the road, bringing the Fiesta to a halt inside. In the evening light she was able to

make out the shadow of a large house at the end of a long, straight driveway. There were no lights on inside the house.

She sensed nothing.

It could have been an empty shell down there.

'David ...' she said quietly, as if the whisper could rouse him at such a distance.

No, she sensed nothing. Yet she had no desire to enter that darkly unhappy place. If only David ...

Edith eased her foot from the brake and drove onwards.

Lawns soon spread out on either side, woods beyond them, and then there were gardens. In the half-light she could not tell if they were well-tended. She gasped – for a moment she had thought there were people standing in the grounds, but she quickly realized that their sinister stillness had the frigidity of stone. She ignored the impression that these statues were observing her approach.

The house grew larger in the windscreen, soon filling the view completely, the car's headlights brightening its façade, but only to dreariness.

She parked the vehicle beneath a tree whose branches overhung the gravelled yard in front of Edbrook, and some distance away from the steps leading up to the house's entrance. A safe distance away, she taunted herself, embarrassed by her own lack of nerve. She regarded the edifice with uneasy curiosity, wondering why it could make her feel so, for still she sensed nothing, no hint at all of its history, nothing of what was contained within those stained walls.

Then why the fear? It was there, deep inside her like some small rotting core, a cancered cell quietly corrupting others around it with almost somniferous slowness, working its way through her system, growing horribly towards fulfilment, encouraged by forces outside ... outside but inside this grim house ...

EASTBURY, DORSET

Imposing, true; but these dramatic gatepiers should act as a warning to those prone to follies of grandeur: Eastbury is now but a fragment of its former self. When built for George Dodington by Sir John Vanbrugh in 1717, it rivalled Blenheim Palace in size and was said to have cost £140,000 – but most has since been demolished. Our interest lies in the fate of one William Doggett, a steward to Lord Temple, a subsequent owner. Discovered in his fraudulent practices, he killed himself, and appears when a decapitated coachman in charge of four headless horses drives up the approach to the house to collect his ghost. In addition, there is said to be a permanent bloodstain connected with his death in what's left of the house, while Doggett himself frequently appears on the drive – and sometimes around the house as well.

In his vastly comprehensive Haunted Britain, *Antony D.Hippisley Coxe relates a hideous coda. During 1845 Doggett's coffin was opened, revealing a body with its legs tied together and a face in the peak of health. This alarming discovery added weight to the persistent local legend that Doggett's crimes continued after death – he was said to return as a vampire.*

IGHTHAM MOTE, KENT

Some ghosts are noted for their violence or cruelty; that at Ightham is more unusually celebrated for its shrewd patriotism. Dame Dorothy Selby won her place in history for warning Lord Monteagle to stay away from Parliament on the day in 1605 that Guy Fawkes and his conspirators intended to blow it up with gunpowder. Some reports have it that the vengeful survivors of the scheme caused Dame Dorothy to be bricked up alive – certainly a skeleton was once found here in just such a condition, adding weight to the legend. Dame Dorothy herself is a restful presence by all accounts, and the beautiful late mediaeval manor house, described as the most complete of its kind in Kent, enjoys a fitting peace in its secluded valley.

So there it was before us. And on initial observation the cottage was enchanting.

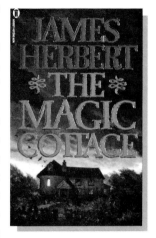

I'd pulled the car over onto the grass in front of the crumbling fence and now we both sat staring at Gramarye, Flora Chaldean's roundhouse, Midge, it seemed, as if in awe, and me – well, let's say pleasantly surprised. I'm not sure what I had expected, but this wasn't quite it.

The building really was round, although the main section facing us was conventionally straight, only one end curving away (we were to understand the structure a little later), and it was on three levels if the attic was included, so maybe 'cottage' was the wrong description. Yet it did look like a cottage, because it was set into a grassy bank which somehow reduced its size. The bank swept around from the sides, moss-covered stone steps eating into the left-hand slope, levelling down to the front garden. There were trees on the rise, some with branches scraping against the white brickwork, and beyond was further woodland (wouldn't you know?). The windows at the front were small and multi-paned, adding even more charm to the general setting, and the roof was of discoloured red tiles.

. . . .

The brickwork, originally washed white but now greying and considerably stained, was crumbling in parts, the pointing virtually absent in several sections. Tiles littered the ground beneath our feet, so I imagined the roof to be pitted with holes. The steps had led us to another door, once painted a dismal olive green and now blistering and peeling, revealing rotted wood beneath. The door faced south and the woods that were no more than a hundred or so yards away across an expanse of tall grass and bramble, a few individual trees dotted here and there like members of a cautious advance party; a clearer area, obviously trampled down over the years, spread out ten or twelve yards from the building, with smaller trees – plum and crab-apple I thought, though I was no expert at the time – standing fruitless (and somewhat dejected, I also thought) closer to the cottage. On this side, because Gramarye was built into the embankment (or rise) the cottage appeared to have only two storeys, and was as round as an oasthouse. The apparent 'ground'-floor windows were arched at the top and Midge had already left me to press her nose against one.

HANNATH HALL, CAMBRIDGESHIRE

(OVERLEAF)

Hidden down a quiet fenland lane is what seems a homely inviting English manor house, but Hannath Hall has quite a history. Indeed, such is its spiritual power that members of the Society for Psychical Research made twelve study visits to the site over a period of three years. Perhaps its condition is due to the legend that tells of a Victorian owner, newly widowed, keeping the corpse of his wife in a haunted room for six weeks, never failing all the while to send meals up to the deceased.

CLAYDON HOUSE, BUCKINGHAMSHIRE

Another example of a haunting from the English Civil War, this time a very aristocratic presence. Sir Edmund Verney was Standard Bearer to King Charles I at the Battle of Edge Hill in 1642. Pressed by the victorious Roundheads he refused to surrender the banner with the brave words: 'My life is my own, my standard the King's.' His enemies soon despatched him, but such was the tenacity of his hold on the standard that they could not remove his dead hand from its shaft: in final desperation they had to slice it from his body. The gruesome tattered lump of flesh was identified later by the bloodied signet ring which, when the gore was cleaned from it, revealed a portrait of Verney's royal master. The loyal fragment was returned to Claydon to be buried, but the rest of Sir Edmund remained missing, and his forlorn ghost appears at Claydon seeking the hand lost in battle.

RUFFORD ABBEY, NOTTINGHAMSHIRE

Did something terrible happen to children at Rufford Abbey in the Middle Ages? Many hauntings here feature children in torment – the local woods have apparently rung with the sounds of the screams of babies in terror, and the local mansion, named after the vanished monastery, reputedly had a corridor which was the preserve of a child murdered while playing hide and seek. Might this be some relic of smothered illegitimate children, sired by mediaeval monks who found their vows of chastity too burdensome to endure? Whatever the reasons, there are more than ghostly children in Rufford Abbey's past. There were monks at Rufford from 1148, when the original abbey was founded by Gilbert de Gaunt, Earl of Lincoln, till the Reformation, when the present mansion on the site of the monastery was started by the Earls of Shrewsbury. Indeed, memorable though shrieking infants are, the most impressive ghost is apparently that of a giant monk with a grinning skull beneath his cowl. It's hardly surprising that local records note the death of a man who died 'from fright, after seeing the Rufford Ghost'.

FELBRIGG HALL, NORFOLK
(OVERLEAF)

Not all hauntings are cruel or dangerous manifestations brought about by the crimes and tragedies of the past. Some rather touchingly reveal a love of the comfort and amenities of home. Here at Felbrigg, seen on a particularly atmospheric autumn day, there is the ghost of one of the Wyndham family, who, when the family house and its contents was bought by a local man in Regency times, returned to safeguard his favourite books in the well-appointed library. A ghost to share cocoa with, rather than fear!

SANDFORD ORCAS MANOR HOUSE, DORSET

If many sites of hauntings feature a lone spirit with neither spectral nor human company to give comfort to its sad wanderings, others have throngs of jostling spirits – and a superlative example of an almost overcrowded house is Sandford Orcas. Within its portfolio of presences it numbers: an unnamed local man who hanged himself; a lady dressed in red silk who for reasons unknown manifests herself on the staircase at precisely 11.50 a.m.; a monk of some kind; Sir Hubert Medlycott, a former owner; and the most alarming of all – the Giant Footman. Seven foot high, this apparition only appears to young virgins, and his unsavoury interest is thought to echo the antics of a huge servant, who either through sheer size or other means of persuasion seduced a goodly number of servant girls. Such was the potency of this ghostly threat that the owners found it well-nigh impossible to get female staff to live in.

MARKYATE CELL, HERTFORDSHIRE

It's ironic that the history of this house should be dominated by two women of opposite characters. Built on the site of a nunnery founded in 1145 by Geoffrey, Abbot of nearby St Albans Abbey, it was renowned in the Middle Ages for the piety of its first prioress, Christina, who had previously lived there as an anchoress. At the Reformation the monastery was converted into a mansion which was later drastically altered in the 1820s to give it the present look of a large Elizabethan pile.

Its notoriety is due to the legend of the seventeenth-century 'Wicked Lady' – Lady Ferrers the highwaywoman. It is said that after her last, interrupted foray, during which she was shot, she managed to reach her home only to die there, and has ever since lurked in ghostly form in the lanes surrounding her family's property. On one occasion she was seen hiding in the branches of a tree – an echo of her habit, when alive, of dropping out of overhanging trees onto her unsuspecting victims on the road below. Other sightings have the errant noblewoman riding at a frantic pace across local meadows or making foolhardy leaps over tall hedges.

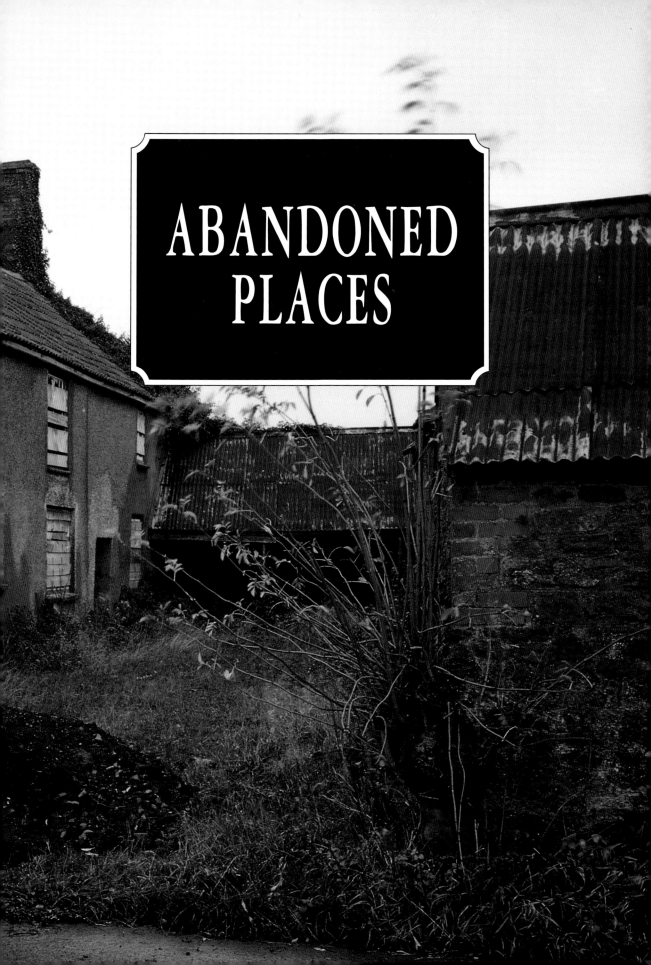

ABANDONED PLACES

In the course of my researches I visit many abandoned places, and they are invariably a source of inspiration. From the city wastelands of my childhood to the shells of ruined dwellings found deep in the heart of forests, I've soaked up their moods and invented stories that sometimes have chilled my own blood.

The bomb-sites around London's St Paul's Cathedral (how did the *Luftwaffe* manage to miss that great hallowed dome?) provided acres of rubble, holes and half-buildings for my very own adventure playground: I had tunnels to crawl through, windows to fire imaginary guns from, hills (of debris) to climb, and catacomb cellars to hide in. (I became used to dark places at an early age).

Then I experienced the Country Holiday Fund, a charitable organization formed to send deprived inner city kids (who, as they lachrymosely put it, had never seen a cow or the sea) to the countryside where foster parents (of a kind) would share their family home with them. I only ever got as far as Rayleigh in Essex and Beccles in Norfolk, but they were countryside enough for me. Here (that is, in those days – things have moved on and developers have moved in since) I found fields and woods to explore, ponds from which to scoop out newts, and deserted railway tracks to hike along. Never once did I feel free though: the household regimes were too strict for that, as I suppose they needed to be. As I recall, the local kids were none too friendly either.

One particular image from that period stays with me to this day (and please forgive the digression here, but it has a point, as you'll see later). It's of a rabbit cull that I witnessed, and my first experience of man's natural but ugly bloodlust and the pragmatic cruelty of country ways (Enid Blyton had never told me about this). I was about nine years old and the people with whom I was staying took me one Saturday evening to a hillside overlooking a field of corn. It seemed as if the whole village had gathered there to watch the farmer cut the corn and I noticed many of the men had dogs with them, and were carrying long sticks, cricket bats, and various types of cudgels. The farmer on his machine cut the corn in ever-decreasing circles and as these became smaller and smaller so the villagers became more excited.

What they were waiting for, of course, was for the rabbits trapped inside to make a break for it. When they did the menfolk sent their dogs off in chase and made use of their makeshift clubs, much to the joy of the other spectators.

The cries of delight when a fleeing rabbit had its skull bashed in, or was caught in the jaws of a dog, amazed and sickened me. The face of my surrogate mother (I use that term in the loosest possible sense – some of these so-called 'carers' took children in for the money paid to them by the charity, rather than for love of deprived children) was something else, a vision of slavering unloveliness. And the smaller the circle of corn became, the more incensed became the crowd. Each rabbit slaughtered fetched a shilling bounty, and the unholy glee on the faces of those claiming their reward, was matched in ugliness only by the blood on their hands and shirts. Yes, I know that's the way of the countryside – I have my own rabbit problem nowadays – but did they have to enjoy it so much? And why was it considered a Saturday evening's entertainment for all the family? The point is, I've never forgotten that bloodlust, nor the special shine in the eyes of those perpetrators and spectators alike. It's an image that's stayed with me all those years, and one I've used frequently in my stories.

Now this is why my digression has some relevance to this chapter, although you might think it tenuous: Years later I visited an abandoned place, a huge gutted mansion that overlooked a round copse of trees; I imagined those dark leaves bristling with unseen life, life that would suddenly erupt from cover to storm across the field, just as those rabbits had burst from their sanctuary of corn all those years before. The thought became part of a novel.

The novel was *Lair*, and the imaginary beasts were mutant rats. The story was a sequel to one written six years before, in which a new breed of super-rat had invaded London, a species created by a sick society whose leaders held scant regard for the by-products of nuclear experiment, and who cared even less for the state of inner cities where such monsters could breed undiscovered and undisturbed until their very power and numbers sent them scuttling into the streets. My idea for the sequel was to have the rats move out from their squalid habitat to the wealthier suburbs, and then into the green belt that adjoins the capital, the idea being that no one was safe from evil created by mankind itself, that privilege was no protection, and even nature had to pay a price.

Epping Forest, the green belt so close to London, provided an ideal analogy, as well as a superb battle-ground, for my premise, and it was a wonderful (and healthy) place to research. On one of my excursions into the forest I came upon that fire-gutted shell of a huge mansion.

This was the remains of Copped Hall and I discovered the tragic fire had happened in 1917. I had, in fact, been searching the area for a suitable lair for my mutant beasts when I'd come across a set of large, rusted gates with lodge houses on either side. The gates were closed but unlocked, so I went through and took the long, pitted road up to the house itself (I assumed I was trespassing, but my attitude on such hunts is what the hell, they can only shoot you).

When eventually I arrived at the manor ruins I knew immediately that I'd found my 'lair'. I also noticed a round copse of trees close by and overlooked by the old house and it was then that the memory of the rabbit cull in Norfolk came back to me.

The lower windows of the house were boarded up with corrugated iron, but I managed to find a loose section that could be pulled aside just enough for me to slip through. Once inside, the atmosphere of abandonment, decay and the ghosts of a greater past sent my mind reeling with possibilities. I climbed down into its rubble-strewn cellars (reminiscent of those childhood bomb-sites) and in the darkness there I found my perfect nesting place for the mutant rats and their Mother Creature.

I spent a happy hour there in the gloom and wreckage, and when I left I came across a quagmire of a yard where corrugated iron sheets had been used to fashion

rough sheds. I peeked inside one of the sheds and discovered pigs lying there in the darkness, a whole nest of them, pink and bloated, resembling the more gross members of my own invented species. It was these animals that had churned the earth outside as they rooted for anything edible, reducing the area to a desolate and naked battlefield and further feeding my imagination so that pages and pages of my notebook were soon filled with ideas for the story. And just how impressive and gloomy the deserted Copped Hall is you can judge for yourself in the photographs on the next few pages.

Such places are not easy to come upon, but an abandoned animal feed mill in Suffolk was another good find. I was researching for a book called *The Jonah* (more of which in the 'Watery Places' chapter) and was given a grand tour of the feed mill by its helpful owner. By then it was empty of most machinery and giant cobwebs hung from high rusty girders like dusty old drapes. We passed through a section where a trapdoor was set into a concrete floor and I was informed that the workings of the conveyors belt lay below. Could I take a look? I asked, and was answered with a firm no. It was alive with rats down there. Oh bliss.

After some discussion, I was allowed to have my way, although the wise owner declined to accompany me. We lifted the trapdoor and I climbed down a metal ladder into the darkness below. I confess I didn't explore too far.

It was like being inside a black, cavernous aviary, for the sounds that came to me were not unlike birdsongs. Only these twitterings were from rats, not birds, as they scuttled around in the darkness like unseen imps, their amplified squeaks echoing off the walls so that they were distorted into a kind of *chirping*. It was weird and unnerving, and I didn't stay there too long; I believe the journey up was faster than the one down.

But such abandoned, neglected – *brooding* – places are a horror writer's dream, and are there for the finding. The joy is in the discovery, and then the application.

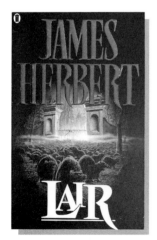

He reached a low, farm-style gate and leaned his elbows against it, a frown creasing his forehead. The ground rose upwards beyond the gate and on the crest of its hill he could see a huge mansion. He assumed it was Seymour Hall itself, but from this distance it was hard to tell the building was a only a shell. He counted six square-shaped chimney-stacks silhouetted against the sky, the building itself having three levels. Only the black glassless windows gave any hint of the ruin inside. But the real cause of Pender's puzzled expression was the land between the gate and the house.

The road leading up to the mansion was made of rubble and the field it ran through was completely barren, the dark earth churned and pitted as though any worthy soil had been scoured away, leaving only the ugly, rock-strewn crust below. It was an unpleasant sight among the lush forestland, and Pender wondered what could have caused such destruction.

. . . .

By now they were close to the gutted manor house and Pender was surprised at its true size. He had only had a side-view as they approached along the track but now, as the rough-hewn road swept on past the entrance, he could see the whole frontage. The large ground floor windows and arch-shaped door were barricaded with corrugated iron, decorated with mindless, sprayed-on graffiti. Rubble was heaped against its walls as though, year by year, more and more brickwork had dislodged itself from the upper floors and formed a defensive barrier around the perimeter. The first- and second-floor windows were no longer black and ominous, for he could see the sky through them, as most of the building's roof was completely demolished. The many chimney stacks were perched precariously on inner walls, rising above the main shell like solemn sentinels. A balustrade ran round the roof-top, joined at the centre by a triangle of grey stonework that stood above the projecting wall of the main frontage. From where they stood, the whole structure seemed to dominate the surrounding countryside.

. . . .

He pushed Whittaker towards the old building, giving one last look at the black vermin streaking across the field. The two men soon reached the piled bricks and rubble which sloped up the side of the house, and they clambered over it, the ratcatcher slipping and rolling back down, the heavy clothing preventing any severe damage. He clawed his way up to the top again and saw Whittaker pushing against the iron sheeting that covered one of the large ground floor windows. The ratcatcher added his weight, using his shoulder to push against one corner of the corrugated iron.

He turned to see the black shapes darting beneath the two-strand wire fence that bordered the field, their bristling bodies momentarily lost in the undergrowth, then bursting forth, racing across the widened track that formed the frontage to the ruin. He stooped and picked up a brick, throwing it at the leading rodent, which swerved to avoid the missile.

Then it seemed as though every square foot of the frontage area was covered in black bodies, the air filled with their high-pitched squeals. Pender began using his boot on the metal barrier just as the first rat reached the bottom of the slope.

. . . .

The blockage suddenly collapsed inwards and he covered his head as the debris fell around him, pushing himself up, thrusting himself through to the floor above. He rose from the rubble like some filthy, bloodied monster from the earth's underworld, scrabbling free, crawling forward, rising on shaky legs and staggering through the burnt-out mansion. The interior walls, disturbed by the fierce down-draught of air, were beginning to crumble, stonework falling to the floor below.

Pender kept going, his movements painfully slow, oblivious to the falling masonry, wanting only to be free from that dark, evil place. He did not know if the helicopter's crew were aware of his presence, nor did he care; he just wanted to be outside. He reached the room into which he and Whittaker had first scrambled in their attempt to escape the pursuing vermin, and made for the bent sheet of corrugated iron. He clambered up the debris to the opening and squeezed his body through, swiftly glancing back to see if he was being followed.

BERRY POMEROY CASTLE, DEVON

Once evocatively mantled in ivy, the now tidied-up castle here still has a tale to tell. Built initially by the de la Pomerois family around 1300 (hence the name), it was substantially altered by the powerful Seymour dynasty in the sixteenth and seventeenth centuries. Nonetheless, it's the Pomeroys who give the place its air of dread. A Lady Margaret Pomeroy lures travellers to a treacherous part of the fortress, from which they plummet to their deaths; she might be the Lady Pomeroy who was walled up alive by a jealous sister and left to starve to death. Meanwhile yet another female Pomeroy has been seen in great distress, perhaps searching for the baby she murdered after it was born to her following intercourse with her own father. To see her is to die, some say. The 'sorrowing' mother may well have been the spectre who appeared to Royal Surgeon Sir Walter Farquhar in 1796: he had come to attend a noble patient, but was horrified to encounter the ghost when shown to the invalid's rooms. True to form, the patient died soon after. It's said that present-day visitors to the site frequently shiver from inexplicable chills, even on bright afternoons.

OKEHAMPTON CASTLE, DEVON

Ruinous in a dramatic, crazily lolling way, the castle has links with one of the most odious women imaginable. A Lady Howard of Fitzford House in nearby Tavistock survived four husbands; in all likelihood she murdered them. Some accounts have her burnt as a witch; all agree on the basics of her punishment. Every night at midnight she has to travel from Okehampton to her old home in Tavistock taking one blade of grass at a time – and this has to continue till all the grass around the castle has gone. In some versions, she does this herself, in the form of a hound; in others she sits in a coach made of bones, driven by a headless coachman, while the hound runs alongside.

CASTLE RISING, NORFOLK

Queen Isabella (affectionately known as 'The She-Wolf of France') conspired against her wayward husband King Edward II in the Middle Ages, forming a suspiciously close alliance with the powerful Roger Mortimer and thereby being responsible for the spectacularly hideous end of her husband at Berkeley Castle in Gloucestershire. His death (by heated poker up the bottom) and her perfidy were tellingly dramatised by Marlowe in his play Edward II. However foolish and ill-advised were Edward's policies, Isabella's ruthless plotting against the man who fathered her son, the future Edward III, left a nasty taste in the mouths of the English nobility, and for her pains she was imprisoned here. Her unhinged shrieks of mad laughter are reported to echo round the still impressive defenses of this immense fortress.

LONELY PLACES

One of the loneliest places I know is Chanctonbury Ring in Sussex – it opens this chapter. Nevertheless – and despite its sinister origins – it's a favourite landmark of mine. I admit I haven't made the long and fairly arduous climb to the top of the South Downs too often, but this copse of trees is visible from miles around and, because it's only some eight miles or so from my own home, it acts as a kind of welcoming beacon when I'm driving back from a publicity tour, a holiday abroad, or even from a day in London. Sometimes, if the flight-path is right, it can be seen from an airplane (nothing finer than *that*). To me it's like a lighted window.

However, the legend goes that this hill on which an Iron Age fort was once built is the remains of a large clod of earth dropped by the Devil when he was scouring out the nearby Devil's Dyke (which I can view from my study window). Surrounded by ramparts of eroded turf, the Chanctonbury Ring is an eerie and menacing place.

Planted with beech trees over a century ago, it stands out dramatically against the skyline, the more so since the damage caused by the hurricane of 1987, which left it gaunt and severe. Inside the ring of trees the atmosphere is markedly chill, and according to local folklore, no birdsong is ever heard from within. From time to time the thundering of invisible horses disturb its natural calm and once in a while visitors swear they have seen an old bearded man wandering around its ramparts (as there are frequent champagne parties up at the Ring, it might be that the old boy is collecting empties).

Incidentally, over the years I've had a great many enquiries as to the location of the actual cottage I used in my novel *The Magic Cottage*. It seems that these readers have been fascinated by its quaint, round shape and its powers of 'enchantment'. I indicated in the book that it existed in the New Forest. In fact, I even placed an ad. in the *Sunday Times*'s property section so that I could use an authentic-looking advertisement at the beginning of the story. I used the fictitious telephone number of Cantrip 612 (Cantrip means a 'wilful piece of trickery: a witch's spell', and the numerals six-double-six, 666, is the Sign of the Beast) and unfortunately scores of would-be house purchasers tried in vain to obtain the number. When the newspaper itself contacted me I had to confess the duplicity.

The truth is, Gramarye, the name of my make-believe magic cottage, can be seen from Chanctonbury Ring itself. It belongs to a friend of mine who is the sister of a famous actor, and because she values her privacy, its exact location must remain a secret.

I constantly use lonely places in my stories because their atmosphere is so palpable and always evocative. It isn't too difficult to create suspense and tension in such locations: a field of cows obscured by a terrible mist in *The Fog*; the tiny isolated mediaeval church in *Shrine*, where the main character meets with a terrifyingly evil force – the church is in Parham, Sussex; the field in which a 747 Jumbo Jet crashes and spirits rise from the wreckage to haunt the town in *The Survivor*; the old crofter's cottage by a lakeside where a hermit who knows the secret of the world's destruction in *Portent* lives – set in the Highlands of Scotland. I've even used Kensington Gardens, oh so cheerless and lonely in the dead of night when the park gates are locked, where the dubious hero of *Creed* is chased by a grotesque who closely resembles Nosferatu, the vampire, as you'll see in 'Capital Places'. And I've used the leafy stillness of Epping Forest in *Lair*, where silence is a precursor to terror – see Paul's photograph on pages 106 and 107. These real places, and many, many others, each with its own special ambience of loneliness, have inspired my tales of horror and hauntings, of terrible episodes by day, foul deeds by moonlight, and sinister happenings at any time.

EAST RAYNHAM, NORFOLK

White ladies, grey ladies, dark ladies – these are quite common. But a brown lady? Altogether a rarer species, but an important example makes her presence felt in this neighbourhood. The local country house, Raynham Hall, contains a nameless portrait of the lady in question. Whoever she was, her spirit delights in tormenting the living. No less a person than Captain Marryat, writer of the classic Children of the New Forest, *met her one night when she apparently leered at him in an evil way, then vanished as he fired a gun at her. Years later, a Colonel Loftus encountered a noblewoman in heavy robes, bathed in an unearthly light, with terrible blank sockets instead of eyes. She does not restrict her activities to the house but likes to glide around the lonely roads near the house, such as this one. Surely she is an even more terrifying creature when met by lone travellers at night, far from the nearest house. Think of those cavernous sockets reflecting whatever pale, unnatural light there may be...*

WINDSOR GREAT PARK, BERKSHIRE

Windsor Great Park is, unexpectedly, a creepy place. Its senile contorted trees take on fantastic forms as light fades – tortured spirits, giants bound in chains, you name it: the possibilities are limited only by your imagination.

It's best not to come across Herne the Hunter. He appears at night astride a huge black stallion, a pack of devilish hounds baying in his wake. Herne was allegedly a forest keeper here in the time of King Richard II. His crime is unrecorded but it must have been a serious one – to avoid disgrace he hanged himself from a tree that still survived in Queen Victoria's time. Herne's appearances coincide with threats to the Royal Family or to the nation as a whole. Some say he was noticed in 1936 when King Edward VIII abdicated and again three years later, just before the declaration of war in 1939. Did anyone see him before the recent fire at Windsor Castle?

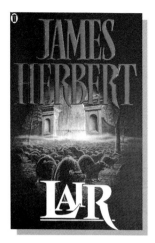

He pulled the horse away from the birch, lifting its head up from the succulent grass. Guiding it back to the path, Denison gazed around him, looking for signs of further damage. A sudden flurry of movement to his left brought him to a halt again. A section of thicket across the path from him shook frantically, then settled into an uneasy stillness. It often happened in the forest – an animal or bird startled by the approach of man, a sudden attack by one animal on another – it was this that made the woodland so alive.

A sudden, spasmodic twitching of leaves and a tiny, almost inaudible squeak told him that a forest creature had fallen victim to a larger enemy. He felt no sympathy, for that was the law of nature, but he was curious to know who was prey and who was predator. He clucked his tongue at the horse and lightly kicked its flanks again. The chestnut took a few steps towards the thicket, then stopped, its neck and legs suddenly stiff.

There was no movement from the undergrowth, not even the rustle of unseen leaves beneath its many layers.

'Come on, girl,' said Denison, irritated at his mount's unexpected nervousness. 'On you go.'

But the horse refused to budge. It regarded the thicket with bulging eyes. Denison became impatient with the horse's inexplicable fear – and fear it was, for the keeper could feel the rising tension in the beast. He knew horses, knew their moods, and he certainly knew this mood. The horse was ready to bolt.

. . . .

Pender began the journey up the long, straight road, constantly glancing into the pine forests on either side. He soon felt completely alone and more than once he turned to see if the head keeper was back there in the distance. He had the same sensation as the day before when he and Jenny had gone off in search of the creatures she had claimed to have seen – that same feeling of being watched. He smiled at his own fears. It was the isolation that exaggerated everything, the quietness of the forest, the leafy screen that hid so much animal life. His upbringing had been in cities, among people, nothing ever still in his vision; here only the breeze seemed to make things move. He froze when he heard a scuffling noise to his right and then dropped into a defensive crouch as something broke free from a thicket a few yards away.

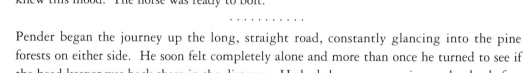

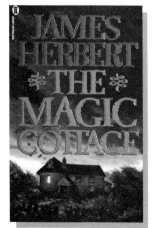

The landscape outside was washed in that special brightness that had nothing to do with warmth, but a lot to do with ice and bleakness. So colourless was the grass that the expanse appeared frosty, and so deep were the shadows beneath individual bushes and trees that they were like black voids. The forest top wore an undulating silver-grey cover, an impenetrable layer over catacombed darkness.

I sipped milk, and liquid cold soaked into me. My eyes reluctantly scanned the dark boundary of woodland, looking for something I didn't want to find. Discerning a lurking figure would have been impossible

anyway, so concealing were the shadows, but that didn't stop me searching, and the knowledge didn't even prevent a sigh of relief when I found nothing.

That relief was premature, though. Because my attention was drawn to something standing midway between the forest and the cottage. Something I didn't remember having been there before.

. . . .

The dusk was fast becoming threatening, the shadows between trees concealing. Branches above us were like contorted arms, agitated by our intrusion, some reaching down as if ready to snag us should we pass within reach; nearby foliage rippled as something slithered beneath its sprawl. There were other eyes inside this forest, and these were wary, uneasy at our presence.

HEDDON OAK, SOMERSET

Now reduced to a stump that you could easily miss, this is one of Britain's most notorious trees. In its seventeenth-century prime, its magnificent spreading branches were strong enough to bear a terrible weight – the bodies of soldiers who fought along side the ill-fated Duke of Monmouth in 1685. Monmouth had been declared King by the poor of Taunton when he landed in Britain to oppose King James II, but his amateur forces were soon defeated, and terrible reprisals followed. A Colonel Kirk and his men, ironically called 'Kirk's Lambs', executed hundreds at Taunton; and of course the infamous Judge Jeffreys oversaw the trials of many others.

The vicinity of the tree is haunted by those who died in agony in its branches. In 1908 the authoress Ruth Tongue, later to write on local folklore, gathered reports of the hauntings, and thirty years later herself heard the sounds of anguished soldiery as she neared the tree on horseback. She was not alone in her sense of alarm – her mount could be controlled only with the greatest difficulty. On other occasions locals have heard not only the sounds of marching but also the appalling gurgles of men in their death agonies. Some have even claimed to experience a kind of throttling as they pass the tree.

NEAR CUTCOMBE, SOMERSET

Tight bends can always be hazardous, but even the most cautious driver may be fatally distracted by the unexpected. After all, there's no provision in the Highway Code for ghostly hearses, pulled by four headless horses without even a phantom driver to control them. Not surprisingly, then, there have been a number of accidents hereabouts that are laid at the door of these reckless beasts. Why this particular stretch of road? Somewhere in the past there must be an explanation, but as things stand, what causes these creatures to appear here remains a mystery...

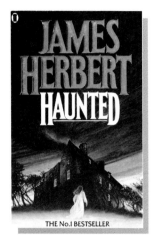

He thrashed through the undergrowth, falling, rising, never stopping, cruel branches whipping at his face and hands, snagging his clothes, concealed obstacles tripping him when they could, birds screeching their own frenzied haranguing. Ash kept running, never once looking back, afraid of what might be following him through the woodland. He pushed by leafy barriers, scrambled over fallen tree trunks, always onwards, fighting through the tangled areas until at last, at long last, he saw a break in the landscape ahead.

With an explosive shout of relief, Ash staggered out onto the road.

He allowed himself a few brief moments to recover his breath, listening for pursuers while he did so. All now seemed quiet back there. Whoever – *whatever*, for he had not stayed to find out – had been inside the mausoleum had not followed him. Nevertheless, he set off again at an awkward jog, his injured left leg dragging, his throat raw from the harshness of his breathing. The morning had lightened, the rain having lost its ferocity, now only a drizzle.

. . . .

The woods were hushed, the trudging of his own footsteps through fallen leaves the loudest sound. And soon he had lost sight of Christina altogether.

He stopped. Looked around. Had he heard someone behind him? He called her name again.

There was no reply, not even her laughter now.

He walked on, only to stop once more.

Had a figure ducked behind a tree to his left?

He waited a moment, but there was no more movement. He continued, becoming annoyed with the silly game.

The noise that brought him to a halt this time was different. It had sounded like a child's giggle.

He whirled and caught a fleeting glimpse of something hurrying through the trees to his right. But it was gone in an eye's blink.

Ridiculously, he thought it might have been a small girl. It had moved so fast, though. He couldn't be sure.

He turned his head, sharply. No, he couldn't have heard the whisper of voices; surely the muted sounds had been a breeze sighing through the woods.

Now the faintest echo of laughter.

Ash drew in a shallow breath. A feeling was rising – was *creeping* – from the hollow of his stomach – or so it seemed – spreading upwards and outwards, a gradual sensory frosting of sinews and nerve lines, seeping through to his outer skin, prickling its surface with tiny bumps. An unease that he could not understand; yet a sensing which he could not ignore. His pace quickened as he walked on through the forest.

Occasionally he would look behind him. Sometimes he would glance sharply to his right, other times to his left. He was not alone. Yet there was no one else with him.

Ash did not run. But he walked in haste.

He heard a snigger, he felt the touch of a hand on his shoulder. The touch could only have been the brushing of leaves. But the snigger could not have been anything else but a snigger.

He almost stumbled, his hand scraping across the rough bark of a tree. He did not linger.

The woods seemed more shaded, more gloomy, as if dusk were impossibly premature. The coldness might well have been in his own mind, for he could feel perspiration on his brow, the clinging of his shirt, the dampness against his lower back. He hurried, now ignoring the small noises that seemed to keep pace with him, the shadows that had no substance when focused upon.

And then he was in bright sunshine, the clearing he had burst into summer warm, as though it had trapped and stored its own heat. He even heard the lazy drone of a blowfly which had found sanctuary from the season's death-chill. His eyes narrowed against the unexpected glare.

The clearing was an orderless area of coarse grass and foliage, with several openings that could have been paths around its ragged fringes. At the centre, its stone walls lichen-patched and stained, stood a small, square edifice. Its door, a tall rusted iron gate with grass growing through the lower bars, was ajar. Two earthenware vases filled with wilted flowers were on either side of the entrance.

He realized that the building, neglected and weather-worn, could only be a mausoleum. A tomb.

GLYDWISH WOOD, SUSSEX

There's nothing more likely to ruin the peace of a woodland stroll than the inexplicable crack of a twig or the heavy weight of sudden birdless silence, descending like a lead cloak to burden the spirits. Is this an insight into our loneliness and isolation, or more alarmingly, a realisation that one has somehow stepped unintentionally into a pocket of malevolence? Rudyard Kipling certainly experienced the latter here, describing it as 'full of a sense of ancient ferocity and evil'.

According to Coxe's Haunted Britain, *the writer on ghosts, R. Thurston Hopkins, was more specific; first he and his party heard an appalling cry, then a colleague came face to face with a creature dressed in tatters, clawing at its own neck while emitting hideous gurgling, choking sounds. This was thought to be the returning shade of David Leary, a farm worker falsely accused of murdering the man with whom he lodged in the 1820s. It seems that the two men were coming back from a sly act of theft when, in the midst of this wood, one suddenly dropped dead. As local gossip had it that Leary was romantically involved with his friend's wife, it was soon decided that a murder had taken place under the concealing canopy of the trees.*

Just before his hanging, Leary told the priest attending him that he would return to 'haunt those people who have hounded me to my death'. After his death it was found that his alleged victim had in fact died of natural causes, and the foreboding and dread that afflicts visitors to this wood is a legacy of that act of injustice.

NEAR REYDON HALL, SUFFOLK

You'll have noticed by now that East Anglia has more than its fair share of ghostly places, and many roads can present the unwary traveller with something he (or she) won't forget in a hurry. This stretch of road near Reydon Hall has seen a terrifying ghostly coach pulled by four decapitated horses, which is said to be under the command of an evil Georgian squire. Such was the power of this spot that a turn-of-the-century horse reared up in fear, throwing his rider and killing him. Other sightings here have included that East Anglian speciality, the Black Shuck – a sort of massive, formless dog-like thing that lurks under the hooves of passing horses. Whatever the reason for these manifestations, the place is loathed by horses, and riders have gone to considerable lengths to avoid it in the recent past.

DARTMOOR

Britain may be overcrowded now, at least round London, but when you are alone as night falls in a place like Dartmoor, you realise that there are still vast and unconquered parts of this kingdom. Dartmoor has always been isolated, a preserve of the elements and, perhaps, of elementals. Certainly few places can vie with it for strange apparitions and disturbing sensations.

Research into the history of Great Hound Tor, to the northeast of Widecombe, has revealed many testimonies to a sense of unexplained fear experienced by those who have been there. Some said that they fell into a sort of trance, almost as though spellbound, only to emerge with a dramatic urge to get far away. The name of the place comes from its resemblance to a pack of hounds turned to stone, but why the air of menace? Did something happen here, in prehistory perhaps, something horrible and brutal? Was the site consecrated to some now forgotten diety who demanded a terrible price? Pure speculation of course, till someone comes up with the answer.

And what can be the reason for the odd occurrences at Merripit Hill, where a spectral sow and her litter of piglets appear? We are told that this brood somehow got to hear of a dead horse nearby and therefore set off to eat it. Sadly they arrived to find nothing left but skin and bones, so dejectedly turned tail back to Merripit Hill, till the fruitless episode is repeated with the relentlessness that characterises so many ghostly events.

Roads crossing Dartmoor have their share of scary resonances. At Shapley Common, for example, there is a point on the B3212 near the River Bovey where an atmosphere of chilliness swamps the traveller and where dogs, sensitive to strange changes in the air, hunker down in abject terror. After such a journey, so crowded with unwelcome paranormal attention, you can hardly blame the lone wayfarer for repairing to a hostelry. But there is no respite – a man who stayed at the isolated Warren House Inn was once appalled to find a chest in his room containing not blankets but a pickled corpse. His shrill pronouncements of 'Murder!' brought a shockingly prosaic response – it was only the landlord's father, sensibly preserved till he could be taken for burial to a nearby town (one account has the cadaver economically lying with salt bacon; not pleasant to hear about over an English breakfast). Dartmoor has any number of contorted rock formations which have given rise to legends of giants, witches, lost battles, people turned to stone – the Spinsters' Rock being one of the more celebrated. Actually this is man made, the weathered residue of a burial mound. The low earth cover of the stones has entirely vanished, exposing the supports of a burial chamber once completely underground.

EDGE HILL, WARWICKSHIRE

The battle of Edge Hill was one of the first great conflicts of the English Civil War; and like all civil wars, it saw fearful atrocities. With the sleight of hand typical of military propaganda, both sides claimed victory, but perhaps the true victor was death – large numbers died on both sides. Many fields of conflict subsequently resonate with the ghostly sounds of combats, but Edge Hill is unusual in that reports of the sounds of warfare occurred as early as the Christmas Eve immediately following the battle. A particularly dramatic trait is the appearance of revenant armies in the sky, wearily re-enacting the slaughter. King Charles I, who sent a Royal Commission to investigate the affair, allegedly declared it 'a sign of God's wrath against those who wage civil war' – the kind of self-serving obstinacy that later cost him his head.

WATERY PLACES

I wanted to find a way of smuggling drugs into the country. Yes, really. A fail-proof, feasible way, but only for a novel called *The Jonah*. This had to be in bulk, so packed condoms inside vaginas and rectums, false-bottomed suitcases, and packages strapped to the flesh were out. Small aircraft can always make night-time drops over the countryside (and they do) providing the pilot knows a friendly but bent landowner, although radar and traffic control is the problem here, as well as adverse weather conditions. But Britain is an island with many miles of desolate coastlines and inlets, with only a short stretch of sea separating it from the Continent. So what better way to bring illicit goods in than by boat? I consulted a map and decided the best area for such illegal activities was the coastline along Suffolk, with its deserted beaches and waterways through which small craft could travel far inland. I packed my bags and headed for Aldeburgh, a small, quiet fishing town on the east coast.

The terrain here can best be described as level, and on 31 January 1953 a storm surge, driven by fierce north-westerly winds, destroyed much of the sea defences along the eastern coastline, sweeping through the flatlands of Norfolk and Suffolk, killing many and leaving hundreds homeless.

That flat and sometimes austere landscape presents a compelling setting for any horror story and inspired what is arguably one of my bleakest novels. An eerie sight was the string of lights along the sea's edge at night, these belonging to anglers, a hundred yards or so apart, who sit there until the early hours, isolated from one another in their plastic shelters, patiently waiting for the fish to bite. Another was the low mist that would drift in from the sea and make its spectral way along the channels. Ideal cover for boats making covert journeys.

Here was my perfect route for smuggling, for these lonely waterways lead miles inland and along their banks stand occasional large houses, good places for 'drops'. With starless nights or foggy days as their allies, the chances of these vessels being spotted by the coastguard are slim. In fact, a friendly coastguard who had invited me into his observation tower explained to me just how difficult it was to catch smugglers. He even affirmed my premise by telling me of the time a large weighted container full of dope had been washed up on the shore after being cut adrift from beneath a boat that was challenged further along the coast.

Great expanses of water are an attraction to me also. Just stand on top of a dam as I did when researching a scene for *Moon*, and you will *feel* the immense power of the deep water harnessed by the concrete barrier, you will *feel* the threat of massed energy straining to break through. Stand by a lakeside on a dull winter's day, as I did when looking for ideas for *Sepulchre*, and imagine what might exist there in the darkest depths and which might one day rise to the surface: '*It might have been the regurgitation of a long-lost island, the waters finally relinquishing their claim. Except it was a living, pulsating thing. A mass that swelled and writhed, a gathering in oozing mud of all those nebulous creatures that men had glimpsed earlier beneath the lake's unsettled ceiling, the forms clinging together as if congealed ... Monsters of immense size were among that curling, viscous mass, while leaner shapes wriggled and clung like parasites, the ascending heap never still, constantly bulging and quivering ...'*

Even a neglected pond can have a perverse kind of allure for me, as in *Haunted:* '*Stagnant water closed over his head, its grip cold and slimy. Ash struggled in panic as weed tendrils clutched him. Clouds of mud stirred and swelled sluggishly so that the moonlight ceiling above was smeared...he saw, sinking towards him through those eddying clouds, a silhouette, a shape whose arms were outstretched, as if crucified, whose flimsy robe billowed and swayed with the currents, whose black hair spread outwards in Gorgonian tresses.'*

And even the warm green waters of the Pacific Ocean can conjure images far removed from the reality. Some years ago I had the pleasure of snorkling through the coral canyons of Australia's Great Barrier Reef, chasing vivid blue and yellow clown fish, avoiding a sea snake that was as curious about me as I was about it, and generally enjoying the sights and colours of that busy submarine world. Yet my mind was instinctively open to plot ideas, and eventually this pleasant episode was converted into one of horror for my book *Portent*, in which a whole section of the reef erupts and millions of coral shards tear through swimmers and fish alike. (Can't help it, I'm afraid, it's my job.)

For the same novel I searched the lochs of Scotland's Great Glen, looking for a remote crofter's cottage in which one of my characters, a blind hermit prophet, could live. This whole region, stretching from the east coast to the west, from the Moray Firth to the Firth of Lorn, is along a massive volcanic rift that divides Scotland in two, and geologists predict that should there ever be a major earth shift along this line, then the waters from the North Sea and the Atlantic Ocean would rush inwards to join together and flood the Great Glen (as *Portent* is about future ecological disasters, that is precisely what happens in the story). It took three days, but eventually I found the perfect site for my crofter's cottage; hidden away beside Loch Arkaig, it looked out upon the long watery expanse that seemed both mysterious and louring in the grim November light.

I'm not sure why these watery places hold such a fascination for me, but I'd guess it has a lot to do with what they might conceal in their shadowy regions. The unknown, in other words, the most potent ingredient in any horror story.

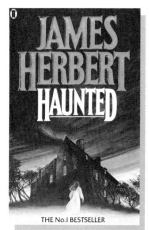

They had reached the knee-high wall and now Ash could see that it encompassed a large ornamental pond, almost a miniature lake, the water stagnant, a murky brown, full of weeds and rotting waterlilies. The sight came as a shock, for although the gardens themselves were not as carefully kept as they might have been, the degenerated state of the pond was surprising.

Ash stared into it, and its sour stench caused him to catch his breath.

He turned to the girl but, unnoticed, she had stopped some distance away. She looked past him at the unwholesome pond almost as if it had come as a shock to her also, that she hadn't realized they had walked this far. There was something skittish in her movement as she backed away.

'Christina...?' he said wonderingly.

Behind him, the turbid water rippled, reeds and tendrils stirred...

. . . .

He followed, breaking into a slow run, reaching the steps that led down from the terrace into the gardens. He searched for the figure in white, certain that he had lost sight of it at this point. Yet nothing moved among the flowers and shrubbery below.

Ash descended and took the centre path towards the pond, eyes seeking left and right. He reached the crumbling wall and looked down on the water, its still surface shiny with moonlight, the silver sheen somehow compelling.

His fascination was broken by the sound he had heard before – the soft padding of footsteps. Only this time they were hurried, and the bare feet were against flagstones.

He whirled around to face whatever it was rushing towards him, but was struck by a powerful force so that he hurtled backwards, the wall catching his legs, sending him toppling.

He crunched his way along the shingle beach, hands tucked deep into the pockets of his black reefer jacket. The collar was turned up to protect the back of his neck from the March breeze which carried with it the chill dampness from the North Sea. He enjoyed the feel of shifting pebbles beneath his feet, the stones at first yielding then joining firmly to resist his weight. The sound was that of a distant army.

. . . .

He passed by the hotel, its exterior brilliantly lit by floodlights. The restaurant, open to view through a wall of glass, was almost empty, the diners existing on separate islands, communication between them restricted to occasional side glances, only the waitresses puncturing their reserve. The summer trade would change all that. There were very few lights ahead: the tiny coastguard tower was in darkness but, just beyond, stood a curious windmill-shaped building, its sails missing, every window lit up. After that, there was only the muddy track leading to another strangely shaped building, a round fortress left over from the Napoleonic wars, this, too, a private residence. The old defensive Martello tower faced water on either side, for a wide river ran parallel to the sea, its estuary several miles further down the coast. The fortress stood on the strip of land that divided sea and river, the river itself

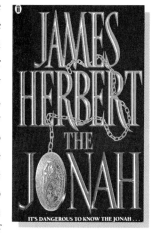

widening out into a natural, protected harbour as it turned inland and cut a decisive path through the marshlands towards less yielding territory. High banks on either side strived to contain the waterway, the waterlogged fields behind them giving evidence to their lack of success.

The ground on which he stood had once been an opening into the natural harbour, but centuries of silt had built up to block the entrance, the locals eventually using the land as it became more firm. Now boats that moored inside the inland harbour had to travel down the coastline and enter through the estuary, avoiding the treacherous sandbanks around its mouth, then wind their way back along the calmer waters. A small quay had been built for the two fishing boats that were too large to haul up onto the beach. Kelso could just make out their bulky shapes among the more elegant sailboats and motor launches as they stirred on the gentle waters. He had spoken to one or two of the fishermen over the past few days, careful not to mention the incident that had dismayed the townspeople a month ago, talking only of the nature reserves in the area and the scavengers that awaited their catch. True to their image, the fishermen were brusque but friendly enough, finding some inner amusement at his questions. They were well-used to ornithologists visiting the many bird

sanctuaries in the area and, if they found him a little different to other bird men they had met, they gave no indication. It would have been totally out of context to ask them about the constant flow of river traffic, whether they had noticed any unfamiliar boats using the estuary recently, but, given time, he would guide their conversations in that direction. And he had plenty of time, it seemed.

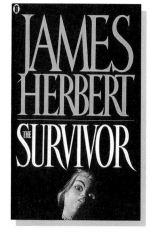

He was startled from his thoughts as his float was suddenly jerked under water. Aha, got one! He grinned and clutched the pipe more firmly between his teeth. He began to play the line, but strangely it wasn't jerking in the usual way. Instead, the line was being drawn steadily down, as though the fish was taking the bait to the river-bed. He began to resist the pull and reel the line in. The rod bent and the line stood

taut and stiff out of the water. Good Lord, he thought, this is a big 'un! Suddenly, the line snapped, throwing him back heavily into the boat. He sprawled there with his knees over the seat, his elbows on either side of the small boat allowing him to raise his head and peer into the misty waters. Just as he began to help himself into a sitting position again, the float bobbed to the surface.

'That's bloody funny,' he said, taking his pipe from his mouth and staring blankly at the bouncing float. 'It *must've* been a big 'un!'

Cursing his luck, he began to reel the broken line all the way in, deciding he'd had enough for the day. It was at that moment he heard the whisper drifting over the water towards him. Was it just one whisper, or had he heard several hushed voices speaking together? Or was it just the rustling of the reeds at the water's edge?

. . . .

He stared down at his feet as he felt a bump underneath the boat, his heart pumping madly, his hands clenched tightly on to the plank seat, the knuckles white from his grip. The bump came again and he spread his feet towards the curved sides, frightened to touch the wooden planking below. Then the boat began to rock, gently at first, building up to a more violent motion. He cried out: 'Stop it. Stop it!' The pipe fell from his mouth, as the rocking continued, the side edges of the boat almost touching the water, threatening to topple him into the murky depths. Just as he thought the boat was bound to capsize, the tossing stopped and it settled back into the water. He began to moan with relief and tears of fright blurred his vision. He felt an icy chill around him, though, a coldness which seemed to sting his flesh.

Suddenly, the boat began to shudder. A fresh cry broke from his lips as this, too, became more violent, and his hands tightened on the seat again. The shaking appeared to be reaching a crescendo, and his vision was even more blurred through his tears and the vibration. Then he thought he heard more chuckling, low, animal-like chuckling with a malicious undertone. But the trembling was running right through him, through his whole gross body, through his brain, until he wanted to scream, to cry out in order to release the terror swelling up inside him. And then, he saw the dreadful thing that nearly stopped his heart, that almost made it burst with the blood rushing through it.

CROMER, NORFOLK

(OVERLEAF)

Supposed to be one of many sites where the dreadful Black Shuck manifests itself, Cromer Beach can be disquieting on a lonely misty day. The Shuck here is particularly virulent; to see it can mean death. The apparition has a variety of forms: sometimes it is headless, with glaring yellow eyes floating eerily ahead of its 'body'; sometimes it has a single eye, Cyclops-fashion, in its forehead. Other variants have red eyes; but however it arranges its constituent parts, the Black Shuck is a must to avoid.

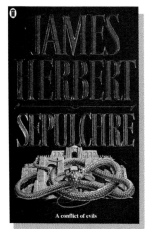

'Can you feel the weight of the water beneath us?' Kline suddenly asked, still looking away from the other man. 'Can't you feel the pressure underneath these thin wooden boards, as if all that liquid down there, all the slime and murkiness that lies on the bottom of the lake, wants to break through and suck us down? Can you sense that, Halloran?'

He almost said no, a total rejection of the notion. But then Halloran began to feel the potency beneath his feet, as if the water there really could exert itself upwards, could creep through those tight cracks between the boards like some glutinous absorbing substance. Kline's suggestion had somehow turned the lake into something less passive. Halloran shifted uncomfortably on the rowing bench.

A ripple in the lake caused the boat to sway.

Kline's attention was on him once more and his voice was low in pitch, less excitable, when he spoke. 'Look over the side, look into the lake. Notice how silky is its skin beneath this mist, and how clear. But how far can you see into the denseness below? Come on, Halloran, take a peek.'

Although reluctant, Halloran did so. No big deal, he told himself, no reason to be churlish. He saw his own shadow on the lake.

'Keep watching the water,' came Kline's quiet voice. 'Watch how it swells and falls, as soft as anything you could ever wish to touch. Look into your own shadow; how dark it makes the water. Yet somehow the darkness allows you to see more. And what if the whole lake was shadowed? What depths could you perceive then?'

Halloran was only aware of the blackness of his own reflection. But the blackness was spreading, widening in tranquil undulations, forcing away the mist as it grew. Kline's voice coaxed him to keep his eyes fixed on the lapping water, not even to blink lest that merest of movements disturb the placid surface, to stare into the darkness until his thoughts could be absorbed ... *absorbed* ... absorbed by the lake itself, drawn in so that what was hidden before could now be viewed ...

'*... There are monsters beneath us, Halloran ...*'

He could see the shapes moving around, sluggish, lumbering patches of greater darkness, and it seemed to him – it was *insinuated* to him – that these were grotesques who knew nothing of light, nothing of sun, creatures who slumbered in the depths, close to the earth's core. Among them were sleeker denizens, whose very tissue-like structures prevented pulverisation under such pressure; they glided between their cumbersome companions, two opposite natures co-existing in a nocturnal underworld. There were others with them, but these were less than fleeting shadows.

Halloran sensed their yearning, the desire to ascend and make themselves known to the world above, weary of perpetual gloom but imprisoned by their own form. Yet if they could not rise, perhaps something of what they sought could be lured down to them ...

The boat tilted as Halloran leaned further over the side.

'*Touch the water,*' he was softly urged. '*Feel its coldness ...*'

Halloran stretched his hand towards the lake that had become a huge liquid umbra, and

there was a stirring below at his approach, a kind of quivering expectancy.

'*... sink your fingers into it ...*'

He felt the wetness and its chill numbed more than his flesh.

'*... deeper, let it taste you ...*'

The water was up to his wrist, soaking his shirtsleeve.

'*... reach down, Halloran, reach down and ...*'

He heard laughter.

'*... touch the nether-region ...*'

Halloran saw the shapes rising towards him, mutations that should only exist in the depths, mouths – were they mouths? They were openings, but were they *mouths*? – gaping, ready to swallow him in ... to *absorb* him ...

The laughter was sharper, startling him to his senses. Halloran pulled his hand clear, standing in the boat as if to push himself as far away from those rearing, avaricious gullets as possible.

Still they surged upwards, climbing as a single gusher, an almost solid stream of misshapen beings, terrible unearthly things without eyes but which had limbs that were stunted and as solid as their bodies, while others were only tenuous substances housed around jagged needle-teeth ... coming closer, rushing as if to shoot above the surface itself ...

... Until they began to disintegrate, to shatter, to implode, for they were never meant for the fine atmosphere of the upper reaches.

HAPPISBURGH, NORFOLK

The gentle market town here has a gruesome past. Centuries ago, one of its chief activities was smuggling, carried out with a devil-may-care ruthlessness towards human life. Certainly this seems the origin of one of the most horrific ghosts in Britain: a mobile torso, deprived of its legs, its head – held on by mere shreds of skin – dangling down its back. This mutilation comes from the waves at night, carrying something hideous in its arms. The explanation? An exceptional act of murder – a sailor or smuggler, surprised by other outlaws in the act of unloading his takings, was killed; then, to make a more portable lump to drag away and hide, his assailants severed his legs before disposing of the body down a well. It's probably these lost limbs that the phantom cradles.

WICKEN FEN, CAMBRIDGESHIRE

East Anglia, riddled with canals, ditches and generally damp and dank places, offers any
number of menacing watery locations. The fiend here is the Cambridgeshire Shuck, a
variable but malevolent 'thing', often black, that appears to the unwary around Wicken Fen
and nearby Spinney Abbey, foretelling the imminent death of someone in the traveller's
family. This wetland area also resounds from time to time with the mellifluous chanting of
the long-dead mediaeval monks of Spinney Abbey itself. Not far from here is a second
dangerous place, the aptly-named Devil's Ditch (LEFT); another lair of the Shuck, it has a
lonely windswept air of melancholy about it even when the Shuck is not in residence.

MERSEA ISLAND, ESSEX

Now much swamped by the twentieth century, Mersea is an ancient site whose history – of fisherfolk, of secret cargoes, smuggled contraband, and of many losses of life to the relentless North Sea – has left a potent legacy. Numerous old houses in the neighbourhood had reputations for ghostly activity, but one of the oldest ghosts is that of a roman soldier, seen many times including a manifestation in the 1970s. It is said that the sounds and cries of ancient warfare have also been heard hereabouts, and certainly the presence of prehistoric human burial sites adds weight to tales of the restless departed from the time before Christianity.

THE RIVER PARRETT, SOMERSET

This is one of many British rivers that have evil associations. At Combwich there is a long-held belief that the river requires the sacrifice, each year, of an adult male, then an adult female, then finally a child. How this horrific heritage came about is hard to fathom, but it may be the echo of a pagan water cult. Apart from human sacrifices, the Parrett has other ghostly resonances. One legend has a local man taking a meal to his mother or grandmother, who had fallen prey to an unknown malady. As he approached the old lady's cottage near the river, he was startled by the terrifying appearance of a massive ebony stallion carrying a rider without a head. Stunned, he stood back as they hurtled past him, then hurried on to his destination. There he found the doughty crone in the liveliest of humours, all signs of disease departed. Giggling with mirth, she told him that 'The Black Man' had taken her enemy, the local witch, as that hag had drowned mysteriously in the Parrett; her spell on the old woman was therefore at an end.

ASHMORE, DORSET

The innocuous-looking pond here is inhabited – by the Gabbygammies. What are they? It's thought they are a sort of ill-defined phantom that for centuries made their home in a prehistoric barrow nearby, not far from the village of Fontmell Magna. There definitely was a belief in a 'presence' at the place – why else would a cross be cut into the barrow's surface? Moreover, inexplicable wittering sounds were to be heard at the barrow, before the road next to it was altered. Precisely why the Gabbygammies then moved to this pond at Ashmore is not recorded: it would be instructive to learn why they chose a watery place after the soily dryness of their earlier home.

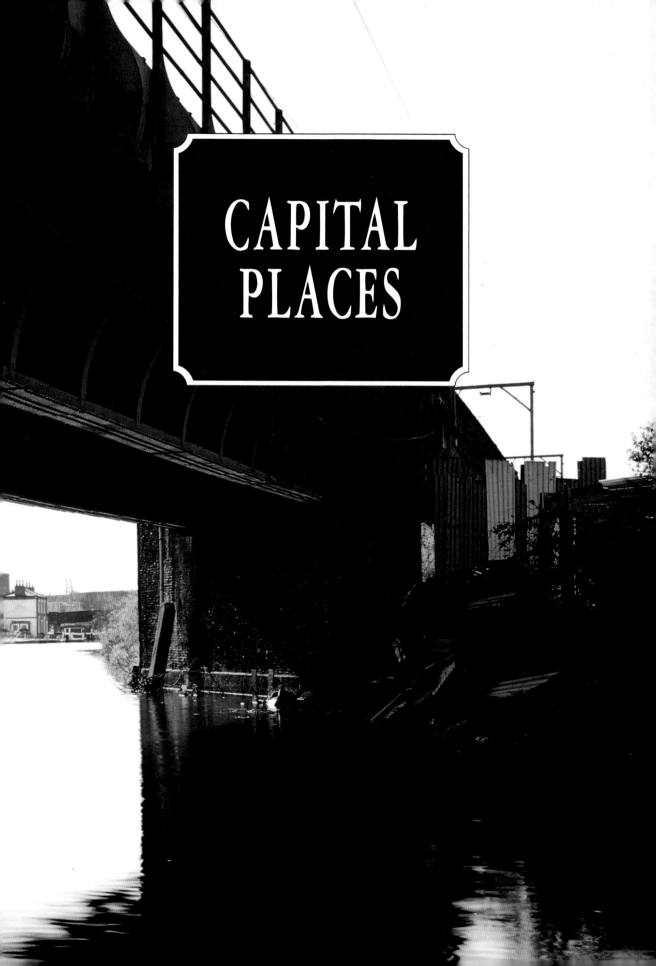

CAPITAL PLACES

Toronto was the cleanest, Jakarta was the most hostile, Glasgow was the drunkest, Adelaide was the most sinister (some very odd murders there); New York had the greatest buzz (the late Andy Warhol sent me champagne), closely followed by Sydney; Nairobi was the most corrupt (I had to hide my own money so that the police wouldn't confiscate it) and Auckland was the most innocent; in its own way Kuala Lumpur was as wet as Venice, and Manila was as noisy as Hong Kong. At nineteen, misspent and broke, I played my one and only chip at the wheel in Monte Carlo's illustrious casino (they'd assumed I was twenty-one) and lost, and at twenty-seven I refused under government edict and machine-gun threat (honest) to have my longish hair cut in Singapore airport, even though John Lennon, that rebel with a clause, had submitted.

So yes, I've travelled and enjoyed the travelling, starting at a fairly early age when such excursions to foreign parts were not quite the norm for someone of my years and social background, continuing through my advertising career and married life. I've had good times and bad times in those places – and many more cities not mentioned – and in all of them I've learned not just about different cultures but about life itself. Yet even though each one has left an indelible impression on me, it's London that I return to time and time again in my work as a writer. My home town fascinates me.

The reason for that is partly because I know it so well, and partly because in my researches I'm still discovering new and different facets, many of which could provide story plotlines for years to come.

Did you know, for instance, that beneath the city streets, and particularly under the Thames, there are hoards of buried treasures, or that you can eat your own sins on Good Friday at St Bartholomew the Great, Smithfield, or that the skeleton and mummified head of the philosopher Jeremy Bentham is still kept on view in a glass case near the entrance hall of University College? Or that Britain's, possibly the world's, smallest police station stands virtually unnoticed inside the base of a lamp in Trafalgar Square, and that there is another tiny police office at the top of the famous Marble Arch gate (which, incidentally, used to be the entrance to Buckingham Palace until it was moved)? Several rivers, although no more than sewers now, still run beneath London, the largest of which is the Fleet. In 1970 a man armed with hammer, stake and spade was arrested in Highgate's Old Cemetery before he could 'settle the Highgate Vampire for good'. Something so horrific, so terrible to encounter, sometimes materialises inside a small top flat at 50 Berkeley Square (it has been described as a slithering mass); it once frightened a young girl into insanity and caused an army officer who stayed overnight to shoot himself.

In fact, there are so many ghosts reputed to be haunting London that their legends could probably fill every page of this book, and they've become a thriving trade for tourist guides. One or two more examples though: St James's Palace is said to be terrorised by a phantom whose throat is slit from ear to ear, while Nell Gwynne's spirit, accompanied by the scent of gardenias, continues to roam the corridors of the

club that was once her home in Dean Street, Soho; 'The Man in Grey' has often been seen in the Upper Circle of the Theatre Royal, Drury Lane, his appearances apparently signifying the success of a particular show and, among a legion of other spectres, Anne Boleyn's headless body still stalks the Tower of London's halls and stairways. All good fodder for the imagination, you'll agree.

However, on a less mystical level, yet even more interesting to me – particularly when I was researching for my novel *Domain*, which concerned the total destruction of London by nuclear weapons – are the thoroughfares *beneath* the city streets. Common knowledge – well, fairly common knowledge, I suppose – is the six-mile-long Post Office railway, which runs some seventy feet below street level, but less known and classified Top Secret by the Ministry of Defence is the network of tunnels and shelters underground. These were originally built for war-time situations and then considerably extended, renovated, and modified during the Cold War paranoia. As well as providing safe havens from nuclear attack, the tunnels are also escape routes out of London. Not for the masses, you understand, not for you and me, but for the politicians and the elite (those with the right connections) of our society. The

main nucleus is around Westminster and the Houses of Parliament and includes, naturally enough, the various ministry buildings in the vicinity and Buckingham Palace – the rumour is that there's a secret underground railway that stretches from this area as far out as Heathrow Airport. So what does that tell you about our leaders?

Walk along the Embankment some time and take note of the various grilles along the pavement. These are air ventilators that serve the network below. On the corner of Westminster Bridge is Queen Boadicea's statue; look at its base and wonder why there should be a discreet locked door set in the stonework. This is just another entrance to the tunnels below. In fact, you'll find many such mysterious vents, air shafts, towers, and odd entrances all over the city. Even the underground train tunnel that runs beneath the River Thames from Charing Cross to Waterloo has a secret sister tunnel alongside it.

No big deal, but it's interesting to know of such a clandestine system, and the more I look into the great metropolis the more intriguing it becomes to me. In my work so far I've blown the city to smithereens, terrorised it with mutant rats, smothered it under a seeping poisonous gas, and sent crazed humans rushing through its streets raping, pillaging, and generally giving the place a hard time. There must be more that I can do to it.

William Blake said, 'Hell is a city much like London', and for creative purposes, I think I'd go along with that.

The old house had been empty for more than a year. It stood, detached and faded, next to a disused canal, away from the road, screened by foliage gone wild. No one went there, nobody showed much interest anymore. A few windows had been shattered by the neighbourhood kids, but even they lost interest when nothing more than silence responded to the crash of broken glass. In fact, the only interest that had ever been shown by others was on the day they took the old woman away...

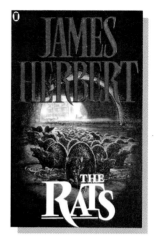

Anyway, it turned out she wasn't dead. A policeman was sent to investigate and then an ambulance arrived and took her away. She wasn't dead, just a lunatic. As far as the grocer was concerned she might just as well have passed on because that was the end of his little number. It had been too good to last.

So the house was empty. Nobody came, nobody went, nobody really bothered. In a year it was barely visible from the road. The undergrowth was tall, the bushes thick and the trees hid the upper storey. Eventually, people were hardly aware it existed.

. . . .

Something moving caught his eye. A dark shape was moving along between the tracks. He walked to the edge of the platform and peered down the track into the gloom. Nothing. Then he noticed the shape had stopped. Realising it must be a rat, he threw the empty milk carton to see if he could make it scamper back into the darkness of the tunnel, but it merely shrank beneath the electric rail. The boy looked up sharply as he heard noises coming from the dense black cave of the tunnel. It sounded like the rush of air, but not the sound caused by an approaching train. He glanced nervously back at the form lurking in beneath the track and up again as the noise grew louder. As he did, hundreds, it seemed, of small black bodies came pouring from the tunnel, some between the tracks, others up the ramp and along the platform.

. . . .

Harris drove through the clutter of military and police vehicles that jammed Whitehall. He was waved down several times by the police and asked to show his pass. When he did, they briskly waved him on, saluting curtly. He threaded his way through to the granite-grey Ministry of Defence building, now the operations' headquarters. The drive through the deserted streets had been eerie to say the least; the only times he'd experienced anything like it had been in the pre-dawn hours, returning from a late-night celebration, when London's concrete canyons seemed virtually devoid of life and the noises of traffic and people were something unreal, hard even to imagine. But even then, there had usually been the sight of another lonely car or perhaps a man on his bike returning from night work. But today there had been nothing. He hadn't even seen any army scout cars that he knew were patrolling the streets, checking that the city was empty, that no unauthorised person remained. For the past two days, there had been a lot of trouble with looters – scavengers who saw the chance of a lifetime to fill their pockets without hindrance. They had been wrong; security had never been tighter. To be in London now, without authorisation, meant immediate arrest

and the whole area was concentrated with police and army personnel with the express task of enforcing the government ban.

. . . .

He turned off from the Commercial Road and drove towards the disused canal, the rats now seeming to diminish in numbers. When he reached the street that ran alongside the old canal, it was deserted of any rodent life at all. He spotted a car halfway down the street and assumed Foskins had beaten him to it. He stopped at the place where he knew the house to be hidden behind a high wall and screened by wild foliage...

He pushed his way through the undergrowth, along the path that had once existed, viewing everything remotely through the glass visor. He reached the old familiar house and stood at its closed front door. Taking off the helmet, he called out again: 'Foskins, are you in there?'

He banged on the door but the house remained silent. Hell, I'll have to go in, he thought. At least, if there were any rats, they'll have all cleared out by now.

He peered through the broken window but could see nothing through the gloom, the surrounding trees and undergrowth preventing a lot of the light from penetrating into the interior of the house. Returning to his car, he brought out a torch from the glove compartment then went back to the house. He shone the light through the window and saw nothing but two old mildewed armchairs and a heavy wooden sideboard. He drew back at the stench that wasn't due entirely to the must of age. He tried to open the frontdoor but it was firmly locked. He then went round towards the back.

What must have been at one time the kitchen overlooked the muddy canal and its door was slightly ajar. He pushed it open gently, its creak the only sound that broke the uneasy silence.

He went in.

ST JAMES'S, GARLICK HILL

In common with many Wren churches, St James's has a history stretching back far beyond the Great Fire of 1666 – the first church here was recorded in the twelfth century. It was, however, in early Victorian times that the site sprang to gruesome prominence, when an embalmed male body, in an extraordinary state of preservation, was unearthed. For some time it was displayed in a glass case inside the church and was affectionately known as 'Old Jimmy Garlick'. He is alleged to have haunted the church as a mute, still figure, eerie and menacing in white robes. It is said that in World War Two, a harassed fireman told him to take cover at the height of the Blitz – but he merely faded away, to avoid the bombs which surely cannot have been able to harm him.

WESTMINSTER ABBEY

*'Monstrous and ghastly pieces of perversity,' sneered Victorian authority William Morris
about the monuments in Westminster Abbey. He and other art critics loathed the way the
pure Gothic church was swamped by 'pieces of undertakers' upholstery': yet that carved
clutter indicates the significance of the church in post-mediaeval English history – a shrine
to the collective genius, or the sepulchral vanity, of successive generations. From Tudor
times on, the building has gradually filled up with monuments to the illustrious dead; it is
hardly surprising, then, that the Abbey has an impressive attendance of ghosts. A cleric, one
Father Benedictus, has been reported in the cloisters; and closer to our times, even the spirit
of the Unknown Warrior has appeared. Further back in history, it was alleged in the
Stuart period that the phantom of an escaped prisoner from the Tower, slain while vainly
seeking the protection of Sanctuary, would appear kneeling as though in prayer and lifting
aloft a hand to ward off the blows that felled him. This blood-drenched apparition, oddly
enough, has not been seen for three hundred years, though the noise of armed struggle has
occasionally disturbed the peace of the site of the killing – the chapel of the choir nearest the
North Transept.*

COCK LANE, GILTSPUR STREET

St Sepulchre's Holborn is remarkable for its late mediaeval tower, seen here rising in a ghostly way above a clear London night as though detached from its foundations. The area nearby was more famous in the eighteenth century for the incessant activities of poltergeists, as well as a ghost ominously known as 'Scratching Fanny' – the possible origins of that name could lead to all sorts of conclusions. It may be that the proximity of Smithfield had something to do with the other ghosts – after all, it was the site of innumerable executions in mediaeval and Tudor times, none more horrific than the burning of heretics, tainting the foul city air with the reek of scorched human flesh long after shrieks of unbearable agony had been dispersed by the uncaring breeze.

There was nothing unusual about clients waiting in their cars until their appointment with solicitor, accountant – or even private investigator – in Gray's Inn Square, but Steadman felt an unease he hadn't experienced for a long time. A throwback from the time he'd lived with that unease for weeks, sometimes months, on end. And it had been triggered off just by the meeting of eyes.

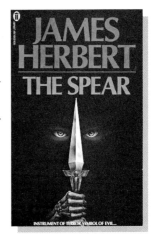

He crossed the smooth roadway and entered the gloomy interior of the red-bricked terraced building that contained his small agency, along with three company accountants' offices. It was a prime position for an enquiry agency, in the midst of the legal 'ghetto', Lincoln's Inn and Bloomsbury on the doorstep, the law courts and the Old Bailey ten minutes away. The address gave respectability to a profession that was often looked upon as seedy, even sordid.

. . . .

Their attitude towards him seemed to change imperceptibly as the hours wore on and answers he gave them matched answers he'd given earlier. They allowed him to shower and dress, then two detectives accompanied him to the agency in Gray's Inn Square where all three searched through recent files, looking for any clue in recent cases that might shed some light on the gruesome murder. One of the questions uppermost in their minds was why Maggie Wyeth's murderer should crucify her to her partner's front door. Could their agency have helped convict someone in the past, and now this lunatic was taking his revenge?

The blackness of the bandstand's base was not as total as Creed had first thought, for now there was an even greater darkness spreading within it. He stared in dismay, then realised

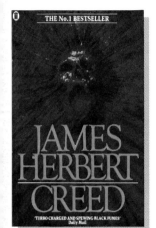

that what he was actually witnessing was the opening of a door; the bandstand itself was obviously built over a chamber of some kind, probably where odd bits of equipment and park deckchairs were stored. The deeper black grew no more. The bald dome of a head emerged first, cast by the moonlight as dull ivory. Creed remembered the intruder in his house had been stoop-backed. The freak came out from the shelter and now its hands, with their extraordinary long fingers and nails, were visible; white and skeletal, they were nasty-looking things. Its huge eyes were almost luminous, as though moonrays reflected on something behind them, giving off an inner gleam; their pupils were like jet-black dots. Its mouth opened and the two long, jagged teeth that touched its lower lip did nothing to enhance the grin.

As it came out into the open, its thin limbs like sticks, their movement brittle yet weaving, Creed could not help thinking of a giant spider emerging from its hole. The analogy was hardly calming.

. . . .

There were trees ahead of him, a dark brooding clump of them, and he knew that beyond was the Albert Memorial, and beyond that the lovely, busy Kensington Gore, where there would be cars and people and maybe even (*oh please Mother of Christ*) policemen.

His pace slowed, his rhythm became even more awkward. His legs became uncoordinated. He ran in the jerky fashion of Jerry Lewis in his prime, stopping, starting, slowing ...

There was something wrong with those trees ahead. He stopped running altogether.

There was *definitely* something wrong with those trees ahead.

Because they were getting closer ...

He was standing still.

And they were getting closer ...

Creed could barely shake his head in disbelief. The clump of trees was moving towards him like a black-shrouded army, their leafless tops swaying as if caught by a wind, their trunks *seeping* – that was the only word to describe the slow but fluid shadow mass – forward.

Creed was soon running back in the direction he'd come from, back towards the bandstand and the two figures that waited for him there, one of them – the stooped one – standing in a clear and glittering patch of grass, thin arms outstretched to welcome him home.

Creed skirted around the Nosferatu clone and tasted the foul air that soured the breeze. As he ran he imagined one of those taloned hands reaching after him. His footsteps suddenly became sluggish, as if he'd hit an invisible boundary where the atmosphere was congealed, dragging at the body, rendering each movement an exaggeration of effort. It was the stuff of nightmares, that frustrating feeling of helplessness, when limbs are leaden and the slow stalking beast is catching up. A battle of wills, no less, between pursuer and prey.

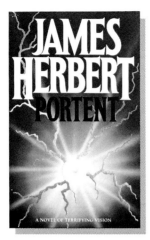

It was drawing towards the end of the lunch-hour and the streets were busy, diesel taxis everywhere, vans, buses and automobiles crawling along at moderate pace. Like a tarnished monument to self-aggrandisement, the Lloyd's Insurance building rose high ahead, its steel and chrome architecture rendered even more unappealing by blemishes and grime. The conduits and piping of the building's exposed 'innards' were in an even more wretched state than the once silvery ramparts, their surfaces rust-stained and blackened. God only knew what was in the atmosphere to cause such deterioration, thought Rivers, but an architect's dream had degenerated into an occupier's nightmare.

. . . .

The trembling of the earth continued, its awful sound almost drowning the human cries. Some drivers and passengers were leaving their vehicles, perhaps wary of becoming trapped inside them, but Rivers stayed where he was, realising what could happen next.

It sounded like a heavy shower or hailstones striking the car's rooftop at first, then larger fragments of glass began to fall. Pieces of masonry and metal bounced off the road and pavements. Larger sheets of glass, popped or shaken from distorted frames, shattered against concrete and bodies alike. His windscreen became an instant myriad of spiderweb lines as a missile exploded against the toughened glass. Still the ground thundered.

Rivers flinched every time something heavy clattered against his metal shelter, yet he was mesmerised by the scene outside. Through the side window he watched the panic as people desperately sought cover, some heading back inside the buildings they had just left, while others clung to anything solid or crawled into doorways. Many lay prone, knees curled up to their chests, their faces buried into their hands.

A man and a woman – the same two he had noticed earlier – came stumbling towards his car. The man, dressed in a beige, lightweight summer suit, shouted something at him, perhaps an appeal to open one of the passenger doors. For a second or two Rivers was motionless, too overwhelmed by what was happening – and its implications – to move. But the terror on the couple's faces galvanished him into action and he reached over his seat to pull at the door handle. His fingers froze on the latch as a huge sheet of plate glass, dislodged from an office tower's upper windows, smashed on to the pavement outside.

But before it had shattered into a million fragments, the toughened glass had sliced into the running man's left shoulder and scythed through the length of his body. Bizarrely, the woman held on to her companion as the rest of his body toppled away, and she looked into the eyes that still flickered with astonished life. The remaining portion of human flesh soon crumpled, leaving the woman clawing at her own face in shocked disbelief.

Glass mixed with blood had spattered the car's windows, a sickening split-second after-effect. He watched as the woman slowly sank to her knees beside the cloven corpse. Another sheet of glass smashed to the ground close by, missing her by only three or four feet, broken pieces flying lethally outwards. Water burst through the fissure in the roadway, a high-pressured fountain that drenched anyone in close proximity. Droplets pattered against the rooftop over Rivers' head.

Below, the wide roadway curving slightly with the river was jammed with scorched, immobile traffic. Another road, equally wide, veered off to the right towards Trafalgar Square. The mist was minimal now, but Nelson's Column could not be seen. Victoria Embankment, running alongside the Thames, was relatively free of debris (apart from vehicles), for the offices on the north side had been set back from the thoroughfare, gardens and lawns between. As expected, the buildings were no more than crushed ruins: the Old War Office, the Ministries of Defence and Technology – all were gone. The Admiralty at the beginning of the Mall should have been visible since nothing obscured the view but, of course, that had vanished too. He briefly wondered if all the works of art in the National Gallery, which was on the far side of Trafalgar Square, had been destroyed beneath the deluge. What significance did they have in the present world, anyway? There would be little time to appreciate anything that was not of intrinsic material use in the years ahead. As he knew they would be, the Houses of Parliament and Westminster Abbey, at the end of the road he faced, had been totally destroyed. Peculiarly, the lower section of the tower housing Big Ben was still erect, sheered off at a hundred or so feet; the top section containing the clockface protruded from the river like a tilted, rock island. And again, surprisingly, only the southern end of Westminster Bridge had collapsed. It defiantly spanned the river, just failing to reach the opposite bank.

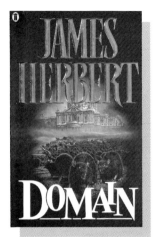

THE TOWER OF LONDON

Since it has been a fortress, a prison, a place of torture and of execution in its grim past, it's not surprising that the Tower is full of dark places. Positive hordes of the unhappy dead elbow through its unlit recesses, its gloomy passages. The ghost of a nameless headless woman, for example, patrols the Bloody Tower – and since hundreds died in the locality, it could be almost anyone. More individual is the presence of Margaret Pole, Countess of Salisbury: she appears punctually on the anniversary of her beheading. Sad, innocent victim of Tudor court intrigue Lady Jane Grey is a more peaceful shade; Guy Fawkes, on the other hand, is said to scream and wail. Finally the pathetic 'Princes in the Tower' have apparently haunted the overpowering, labyrinthine structure, their lives snatched in scurrilous circumstances that may never be properly explained.